Carving Spoons

by Shirley Adler
with Historical Notes by EJ Tangerman
and Harley Refsal

Fox Chapel Publishing Co., Inc.
1970 Broad Street
East Petersburg, PA 17520

Publisher: Alan Giagnocavo
Project Editor: Ayleen Stellhorn
Desktop Specialist: Robert Altland, Altland Design
Cover Photography: Robert Polett

ISBN# 1-56523-092-2

To order your copy of this book, please send check or money order
for cover price plus $2.50 shipping to:
Fox Books Orders
1970 Broad Street • East Petersburg, PA 17520

A friendly tip for woodcarvers

We would like to pass along information on the best deal we have ever seen for woodcarvers.

The National Woodcarvers Association is a non-profit organization dedicated to the art of woodcarving. Members receive six issues of "Chip Chats" a colorful magazine full of techniques, show happenings, photographs of masterworks and more.

We highly recommend that every carver from beginner to professional join - you won't be disappointed!

Membership is only $11.00 per year ($14 outside the USA)
National Woodcarvers Association
7424 Miami Ave.
Cincinnati, OH 4543

Acknowledgements

It is fun to think back in time and surmise just what events or personal interactions led me to be where I am today. It is impossible to name all those who gave a word of encouragement ... or a swift kick ... when it was needed. To all of you, my thanks.

There are a few people directly connected with this book that I would like to thank.

Pam Johnson of Mountain Woodcarvers in Estes Park, Colorado, who prompted the idea for this book. Pam, you are a true visionary.

Alan, Ayleen and the staff at Fox Chapel for the opportunity to do this book.

E.J. Tangerman and Harley Refsal for their contributions to the history section.

Most of all, thanks to my husband Steve for his support during this project and his time and effort to shoot the photos. I hope we get to work on projects together for many more long years.

Dedications

I would like to dedicate this book to two very special people. My mom, Waldorene Pigg, and my uncle, Van Dowda.

Mom always led me to believe I could accomplish anything I set my mind to. Because of her positive attitude, I have tried many things and had many wonderful experiences. What a great gift for a parent to give a child! — "Thanks, Mom."

My uncle Van contributed patterns and chip carved spoons to this book. He sent me my first box of spoon blanks. From that box came hours of carving pleasure, new skills and confidence and ultimately this book.

Van has unselfishly shared his enthusiasm and knowledge. It is a fitting tribute to him that through this book, the enjoyment of spoon carving can be shared with others and will go on and on. — "Van, keep my chair open on the porch and the broom handy."

Table of Contents

Foreword

There is only one good reason for writing this book—to pass on some of the enthusiasm I have for spoon carving. And I have plenty to spare!

Spoon carving is the perfect carving project for someone who has never carved before. I know this to be true because as a beginning carver, I received a box of spoon blanks in the mail one day—no pictures and no instructions. I have been hooked ever since. Just think about it.... Your finished piece doesn't have to look like a person, a rabbit or a dog. It just has to look like a spoon.

Spoon carving is also enjoyable for someone who has years of carving experience. The possibilities in handle design are endless and can be as complicated as your imagination will allow. The challenges of completing a detailed design in hardwood can be formidable, yet extremely rewarding.

Spoon carving requires very little wood, few tools and no permanent workspace. You can carve spoons almost anywhere. So let's get started. Don't look for practice work in this book. After a brief introduction to the history of spoon carving, we are going to jump right in and begin carving a spoon. Why postpone the fun!

Shirley Adler

The History of Welsh Love Spoons
by E. J. Tangerman

Skilled men, even in primitive times, made presents for their girlfriends and more so for their wives. Less-skilled men hired the skilled ones to produce presents for the opposite sex. Remember, the troubadour sang to his lady love; the crow-voiced male hired the troubadour to serenade his lady for him. Gallants through the ages have offered "love gifts" to ladies and frequently to more than one. Coquettes, through those same ages, have collected love tokens from naive swains. In modern times, such tokens are often commercially manufactured, but the tradition remains. And the man who has made something for his wife and his home, whether it is kitchen tools, furniture or a piece of art, is satisfied, honored and respected.

This tradition was not one-sided; the lady in question also made things for the man. They might have been clothes, meals, decorative objects or just a home, but they were done by hand, out of love. In ages past, the people involved were most often rustic rather than urban dwellers and often illiterate or tongue-tied because they had more hand skills. And many of the men were sailors or others who were required by their work to be away from their loves.

Being enamored with these tokens myself, I was much impressed in 1949 by a slim volume from England titled *Treen*, by Edward H. Pinto. It was a sort of dictionary of his collection of the 2,000 objects he called "wooden bygones," each identified by whatever provenance he and his wife could discover. Most were household and personal objects; all were handmade. In 1959, a second edition was published about his collection, now grown to 7,000 pieces. It reported that a number of collectors had been discovered through the first edition—people who had searched out handmade wooden objects for the home, kitchen, boudoir and even the barn.

Being handmade was a vital aspect of the objects in Pinto's collection; machine-made things were not permitted. It also indicated clearly the division in Great Britain between classical, or formal, woodcarving, which was done by professionals for churches, public buildings and formal homes, and the much smaller and intimate items and tools that were whittled and carved by peasants, particularly from the seventeenth through the twentieth centuries. In that second edition, only one seven-page chapter and three or four pages of pictures are devoted to "Love Spoons and Other Love Tokens." Many of the other chapters include objects that were made for love and utility. But it is the love spoons that have survived and been reborn in the present century.

The spoon and the bowl are undoubtedly two of man's oldest tools, because, with the knife, they are essential to man's existence. As such, they were treasured and decorated. Further, they were carved by men, because in primitive tribes, the carvers were all male. (I have visited primitive tribes where the carver still ranks with the shaman, medicine man or even chief because of his skill, often considered a gift from the gods.) The word spoon comes from the old English *"spon"* meaning a chip or block of wood of the right size to make a spoon or ladle. So it is logical to assume that "love spoons," minus the valuable commercial name, have existed for millennia. We can't say for sure, however, because wood rots and breaks.

The oldest carved spoons still extant are from Egypt. They date back to 1250 BC and were used for ointment. The Vikings carved paired spoons integral with a connecting chain a thousand years ago. Welsh carvers began carving their decorated ones in the seventeenth century according to their claims (the earliest one extant is dated 1677), and they apparently invented the name and a lot of the traditions. They carved such spoons though the 1700s, 1800s and 1900s starting with simple designs that gradually led to more and more florid (and less useful) larger spoons. Many nineteenth century spoons are notable for the time they took to carve, not their art. Also, the many Welsh males who were not skilled with their hands commissioned their more skilled brethren to carve spoons for them. Further, as is usual with such efforts, the sentiment and effort were commercialized so that the love spoon became less a bond between swain and hoped-for bride than a sort of token, like the fraternity pin when I was in college. Attractive young ladies accepted them from available suitors for their collection. Then love-spoon making practically died out.

It was revived in the present century as a craft producing souvenirs for tourists, and many present-day spoons are largely produced on machines. Carved spoons—call them love spoons if you wish—were produced in Sweden, Switzerland, Germany, Britain and Yugoslavia. I have heard that in Sweden, the man courting wore a spoon in his buttonhole and the courted lady wore a yarn doll. If they agreed, they exchanged tokens. Apparently, a similar custom was observed among Britons. And love spoons in vast variety, mostly ornate, were carved all over England. I have sketched some examples of these ancient spoons from some in museums. But most are long-gone, because wood is not everlasting (and neither is love).

The Welsh love spoons apparently began as a simple adaptation of several ancient whittling tricks and were relatively small, about the size of a teaspoon. The handle was a ball in a cage and there might or might not be several links on the upper end. There were usually two balls in the cage, suggesting that the two live together—or sometimes only one to suggest that the carver's heart was enthralled by the lady. Some modern interpreters say the balls suggest the number of children hoped for, with a larger ball the boy and a smaller one the girl. This strikes me as far-fetched, because if one ball were visibly smaller than the other it might well drop out. Better is the old belief that the chain links on the end of the handle suggested the number of hoped-for children.

As the years passed, the love spoon became more and more elaborate, as is common with any kind of primitive art. Handles were broadened to become surfaces that could carry a carved design in relief or even scroll-sawed and pierce-carved designs. The spoons became less practical and more purely ornamental. They might carry initials or a word like *cymru* (love), but strangely never a better Welsh word, *cariou* (darling). Some were very fragile filigrees, which probably would have disintegrated when dusted, even if enshrined on a wall. Chip carving, a very old form of carving that involves making patterns with triangular or diamond-shaped depressions with a sharp knife, was also used to decorate love spoons.

The spoon or ladle (in Wales it's a "carved spoon") did not remain a straight or slightly bent-handled tool; ingenious carvers bent, distorted, thickened, thinned and angled the handles, created pierce-carved scenes in a triangular space created by extending the handle down level with the spoon base, and so on. It is almost hopeless to attempt to describe the many shapes developed. I've drawn sketches of some of the more unusual ones in museum collections in Europe.

Woods used for love spoons were as varied as the designs. The Scandinavians tended to use pine or fir; the Welsh began with sycamore but widened their selection later to include cherry, walnut, yew, apple, oak and even beech. Modern spoons are often mahogany, walnut or pine; in the Pacific they may be Macassar or regular ebony or other hardwoods. It depends on the carver and how hard he is willing to work for the lady. If she is a flirt, pine is good enough.

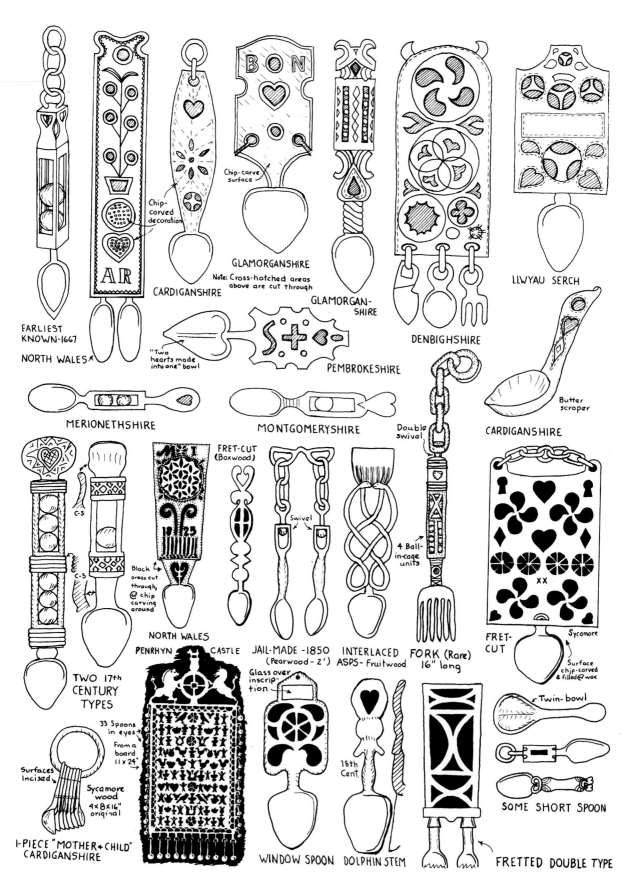

EARLIEST KNOWN-1667
NORTH WALES

CARDIGANSHIRE

Chip-carved decoration

Chip-carve surface

GLAMORGANSHIRE

Note: Cross-hatched areas above are cut through

GLAMORGAN-SHIRE

DENBIGHSHIRE

LLWYAU SERCH

"Two hearts made into one" bowl

PEMBROKESHIRE

Butter scraper

CARDIGANSHIRE

MERIONETHSHIRE

MONTGOMERYSHIRE

Double swivel

TWO 17th CENTURY TYPES

C-S

C-S

NORTH WALES
PENRHYN CASTLE

Black areas cut through, @ chip carving around

FRET-CUT (Boxwood)

Swivel

JAIL-MADE -1850 (Pearwood-2')

Glass over inscription

INTERLACED ASPS- Fruitwood

4 Ball-in-cage units

FORK (Rare) 16" long

FRET-CUT

Sycamore

Surface chip-carved & filled @ wax

Twin-bowl

SOME SHORT SPOON

Surfaces Incised

33 Spoons in eyes
From a board 11 x 24

Sycamore wood 4 x 8 x 16" original

1-PIECE "MOTHER + CHILD" CARDIGANSHIRE

WINDOW SPOON

18th Cent.

DOLPHIN STEM

FRETTED DOUBLE TYPE

© E.J. Tangerman, used by permission

The most prolific spoonmaker of my acquaintance is Holger Jensen of Clifton, NJ. His carving has all been hobby-related - he has been mentioned in a book on carousel horses and has exhibited hundreds of whittled pieces of all sorts - but his abiding interest is love spoons. A number of his designs are shown here, and he admits to carving several hundred.

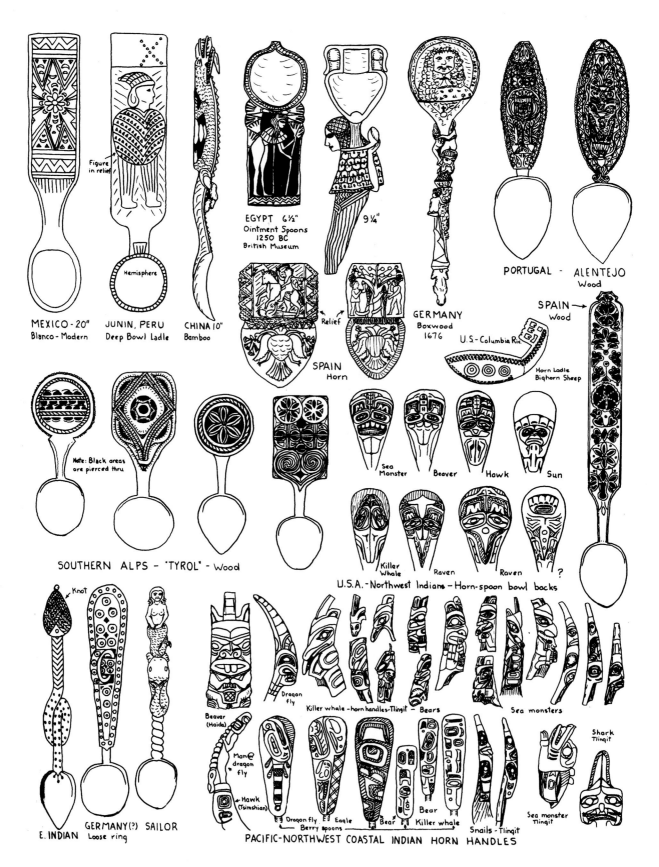

EGYPT 6½"
Ointment Spoons
1250 BC
British Museum

9¼"

PORTUGAL - ALENTEJO
Wood

MEXICO - 20"
Blanco - Modern

JUNIN, PERU
Deep Bowl Ladle

CHINA 10"
Bamboo

Figure in relief

Hemisphere

Relief

SPAIN
Horn

GERMANY
Boxwood
1676

SPAIN →
Wood

U.S - Columbia Riv.

Horn Ladle
Bighorn Sheep

Note: Black areas
are pierced thru

SOUTHERN ALPS - "TYROL" - Wood

Sea
Monster

Beaver

Hawk

Sun

Killer
Whale

Raven

Raven

?

U.S.A. - Northwest Indians - Horn-spoon bowl backs

Knot

E. INDIAN

GERMANY(?)
Loose ring

SAILOR

Beaver
(Haida)

Dragon
fly

Man @
dragon
fly

Hawk
(Tsimshian)

Dragon fly
Berry spoons

Eagle

Bear

Bear

Killer whale

Killer whale - horn handles - Tlingit - Bears

Sea monsters

Snails - Tlingit

Sea monster
Tlingit

Shark
Tlingit

PACIFIC-NORTHWEST COASTAL INDIAN HORN HANDLES

© E.J. Tangerman, used by permission

6

Carving Spoons

Love spoons, or at least decorative spoons for ladies, have been made in other materials, like horn or bone. And they have been made in sets. I've seen Dutch spoons with carved handles hung on a rack for kitchen display, German spoons and forks with grape branches and leaves on handles and tiny Chinese spoons with elaborately carved handles, probably used with ladies' snuff bottles of stone. In Thailand and Burma, they made spoons of bowl-shaped shells with conch-core handles riveted in place and carved with designs. I even bought a number of elaborate ladles in northern Siberia carved with traditional designs. The point is that designs are endless and materials are whatever is available. (Incidentally, it is obvious that earliest spoons were wood rather than metal because it could be formed by peasant tools. Also all European manor houses and castles had live-in craftsmen familiar with wood.)

Much of the symbolism now in Welsh tourist booklets sounds suspiciously like modern inventions to boost sales. In addition to the symbolism of the ball in a cage and the chain mentioned earlier, some of the major symbols are: hearts and twin hearts, anchors, ropes, cables, even ships, locks, keys, miniature houses, elaborate chain links and the Chinese Yin and Yang (like commas interlaced). Then there are lovers' and other knots. Vines, local birds, animals and flowers are all rather obvious in sentiment—you can make up your own symbolism for them. Others, like the acanthus leaf (growing love), bells (wedding), cross (religious connotations), diamonds (promised wealth), twin bowls (togetherness), horseshoe (good luck), lanterns (lighting the path), spade (willingness to work) and spectacles (good luck or long life together or even "I like what I see") all breathe respect, love, domesticity, safety and happiness. The whole idea suggests a spoon-fed existence that seldom materializes. After all, the first tool with which a child becomes acquainted is a spoon, and the last an elder is fed with is a spoon, which is a symbol in itself.

A study of the sketches will indicate that the symbolism is endless—or at least the modern interpretations are. Many of the designs were probably just traditional ones copied from older objects, in some cases by carvers who were illiterate and so could "read" only the symbolism. Much has been added by modern pseudo-savants or by entrepreneurs seeking to enhance a sale. Even the spoon form was not sacrosanct—some carvers depicted knives and forks or other objects they thought might be appealing.

There are (or were) many local symbol differences, of course. Present-day souvenir carvers swipe ideas from other areas with impunity and will carve any old idea a customer offers. In the British Isles, for example, dolphin-shaped or crooked spoon stems were originally from Caernorvanshire, the keyhole and heart were from Penbrookshire, and so on. Carvers from some areas stressed fretsaw work and chip carving. Others did intricate detail carving. Still others did whittling stunts, as will be seen from the sketches. And the enthusiasm of the carver may go overboard—the large spoon from Penrhyn Castle, for example, was carved from a thin 11" x 24" board and has hooks around the sides and bottom for 31 separately carved spoons! If the lady being courted started to interpret that, she'd have left the swain flat—or started an orphanage. The wooden chain incorporated in some carvings could have meant more than a wedding—some were carved in prison. Occasional wide-handled spoons (usually from North Wales) had designs filled in with colored wax in the manner of the scrimshaw done on ivory by our West Coast Indians. An occasional spoon incorporates a small mirror—an ancient protection against the evil eye, even in Wales.

Incidentally, Welsh carvers commonly boil either the blank or the finished spoon to rid it of sap and prevent checking, adding salt to the water if they want to bleach the spoon in the process. Others rub salt on later as a bleach. Finishing is usually accomplished with linseed oil for decorative spoons or vegetable oil if the spoon is to be used. The bowls must, of course, be carefully sanded before finishing to avoid rough spots and burrs. But the usual modern spoon is decorative only, so it is possible simply to rough-shape the bowl. I've seen some that show the gouge marks clearly.

An Introduction to Scandinavian Spoon Making
by Harley Refsal

Most of us in the Western World can't imagine, nor have we ever even stopped to think about, a time when people didn't have spoons. The very first bites of non-liquid food that go into our mouths as babies are lovingly placed there with a spoon. And from those very first spoonfuls on, spoons continue to serve as essential utensils around the home. Spoons are so commonplace that we have probably never thought much about where they came from or how they developed.

Mankind's first and oldest utensil and tool is the knife. Knives have been around for thousands of years. Early examples were formed from stone, and when people began working metal, knives appeared in bronze, iron and, finally, steel. People not only hunted and defended themselves with knives, they ate with them as well. Thus, knives were our earliest eating utensils, handy improvements on earlier methods of eating meat, which undoubtedly consisted of gnawing meat off bones or eating with one's fingers.

Skipping over the second utensil, the spoon, we can briefly mention man's third and newest eating utensil of the Western World, the fork, which was not widely used by common folks until quite recent times. Wealthy people on the European continent used forks, but at least in some parts of Europe (Scandinavia, for instance) the use of forks as eating utensils was not widespread until well into the 1800s.

Throughout the ages, eating utensils developed to accommodate what one ate. In Norway and Sweden the main fare until the mid-1700s consisted primarily of a grain-based gruel, or porridge, cooked simply in water—no milk, no sugar, no raisins—just grain, boiled in water. This gruel was typically served in a large common bowl from which people dipped and ate.

A marked improvement over simply dipping one's fingers or a piece of bread into the gruel was the use of a shaving of wood, something like the wooden spoons that accompany small, individual, cardboard ice cream containers today. In fact, in the Norwegian language, the word for a wooden shaving or wood chip is *spon* (pronounced SPONE to rhyme with CONE), the parent word for our English word spoon. Shavings, including ones large enough to use as a primitive spoon, would have been readily available in the pre-18th century Norwegian home, as woodworking of many types would have been done right in the main room of the house. Chips resulting from chopping firewood were undoubtedly used as early spoons as well.

From those humble origins—using shavings or wood chips from other woodworking projects—spoon-making as an end in itself gradually developed. The word for spoon in modern Norwegian is *skje* (pronounced SHAY). A ladle or larger spoon, such as a serving spoon, is a *sleiv* (sounds something like SLAVE). Both the words skje and sleiv originate from the process of splitting, cleaving or riving a branch lengthwise. The branch chosen for splitting, from which a spoon would be carved, was typically slightly bent, thus providing a natural bend for the utensil's handle.

"Spoon gouges" or curved-bladed knives developed to hollow out the spoon, while a common whittling knife was used to shape and carve the rest of the spoon. True to the spirit of folk art, decoration of these practical objects soon followed, and handles often became longer, wider and flatter in order to accommodate the wide variety of carved and incised decoration that began to emerge.

Eventually each family member had their own spoon, with which they ate, then licked clean and, finally, stuck in a crack, handle end in, between the logs of the log house. The spoon was thus "clean" and ready for use at the next meal. Visitors took their own spoons along.

It wasn't until well into the 19th century that the tradition of furnishing guests with spoons, rather than having them use their own spoons that they had brought with them, began to emerge. And that new custom was not without its problems. In the days when each guest furnished his or her own spoon, only one person used each spoon, and the passage of germs was kept to a minimum. But communally used spoons demanded proper dishwashing techniques between users, something that was not quite perfected yet. Word had reached rural communities that one should wash eating utensils before someone else used them, but soap, and even hot water for that matter, was often neglected. So many people's experiences with eating from someone else's inadequately washed spoon led to a good deal of sickness, something that certainly must have convinced many a traditionalist that these new-fangled fads weren't all they were cracked up to be.

Young men often created highly decorated spoons and presented them to young ladies as suitor gifts. At weddings, wedding spoons (two carved wooden spoons connected at the ends of their handles by a chain, all carved from one piece of wood) were sometimes used by the bride and groom while eating a special festive porridge.

As mentioned above, spoons were made not only of wood, but of metal, especially silver. While wooden spoons could be made by almost anyone and were therefore most common, spoons of silver had to be made by craftsmen who possessed more experience and specialized equipment. Silver was obviously more costly as well, compared to wood, which was free, so only relatively well-to-do people owned and used silver spoons.

Spoons were also fashioned from horn, especially cow horn. When heated to about 320 degrees Fahrenheit, cow horn becomes very pliable and can be formed into a variety of shapes, including spoons. Forms for making spoons were made from wood or metal, and the heated, softened horn was pressed into shape, trimmed and polished.

The Sami people (formerly referred to as Lapps) of northern Norway, Sweden and Finland, as well as the Kola Peninsula of Russia, have a long and rich tradition of making objects, including spoons, from reindeer horn. The distinctive shape of Sami spoons, together with their unique scrimshaw-like designs, make them highly desirable souvenirs.

In summary, spoons, the Western World's second oldest eating utensil, have humble origins. But they have emerged as highly versatile household objects. Spoons are used when we take our first bites of food as infants, when we celebrate special occasions, when we eat that late-night snack. Spoons are fun to make and decorate, and a handmade spoon is sure to give pleasure to maker and user alike.

Chapter One
Spoon Carving Basics

Tools

Basic spoon carving requires very few specialized tools. A good quality knife and a spoon gouge are all you need to get started. More intricate spoon handle designs and very hard wood may necessitate additional tools to make your carving task easier and achieve the results you want. But to begin with, the tools you see in the photo below will serve you well for the spoon carving projects in this book.

Hundreds of carving knives are available at local carving supply stores and through mail order catalogs. Finding a knife that fits you is as important as wearing a good fitting, comfortable pair of shoes. Shop around and look for a knife that "feels" good in your hand and has a blade that will accomplish the type of carving you want to do. Always buy the best quality tools you can afford and keep them sharp.

The spoon gouge is curved to allow you to reach deep into the bowl of the spoon. Spoon gouges come in a variety of blade widths and sweeps. Blade widths are measured in millimeters. The sweep is the curvature of the blade of the gouge. An 8mm with a #5 sweep pictured here is a good size if you are going to buy only one gouge. You may want to purchase others as you get more proficient at spoon carving.

There are some chip carving designs included in this book. Chip carvers generally use a chip carving knife and special techniques to remove wood in single-piece chips. If you'd like to try your hand at a chip-carved spoon, you'll need to purchase a chip carving knife. There are many good books on chip carving, and some reading

A good quality knife and spoon gouge are all you need to begin spoon carving.

before you tackle this carving style will save you a lot of frustration.

In general, when thinking about buying any kind of carving supplies, it is best if you visit and get to know the people who run your local woodcarving shop. You can see the tools and perhaps try them before you buy. Carving shops are a wonderful source for information, tips, classes, shows and new friends. If there is not a carving supply shop near you, then wood, books, and carving and sharpening supplies can be mail ordered. Woodcarving magazines, such as *Chip Chats*, a publication of the National Woodcarvers Association, are available at many bookstores and list mail order sources.

Sharpening

New tools need to be sharpened. Don't think that because a knife or gouge is new it is ready to use. This is never the case. Sharpen your own tools or ask another woodcarver or professional sharpening service to help you. If you feel you need to learn about sharpening, there are many good books available on sharpening tools. My suggestion would be to read several books and develop techniques that suit you and your tools.

Once you have a properly sharpened tool in your hand, whether it was sharpened by you or a fellow carver, learn what it can do and what it feels like—then accept nothing less. Carving with dull tools takes all of the pleasure out of the carving experience. It is also very dangerous because you cannot predict how your tool will react to the wood.

Safety

I use a carving glove and recommend them to anyone, especially beginning carvers. The carving gloves I use are knitted from Kevlar™ or stainless steel thread and are available from local carving supply stores or through mail order catalogs. To protect yourself from cuts, you should buy one for the hand opposite your carving hand. For example, if you hold a carving knife in your right hand, buy a glove for your left hand. They are quite comfortable and will protect you from slicing cuts. I have been spared at least two trips to the hospital.

In addition, you should keep in mind the general safety rules for any type of carving, including keeping your tools sharp, follow the manufacturer's directions for use of power tools, and use good ventilation when applying finishes.

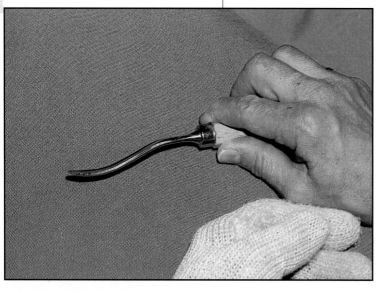

The spoon gouge is curved to shape the spoon bowl. An 8mm spoon gouge with a #5 sweep is a good tool for many spoons.

Using common sense when carving will help you avoid many unnecessary accidents and allow you to enjoy carving to its fullest extent.

Wood

I urge beginning spoon carvers to use basswood for their first projects. Other names for basswood are lime or linden. The scientific or botanical name for the common United States species of basswood is *Tilia americana*. Basswood is typically a very light-colored wood with a small and even grain. It is one of the softest of the hardwoods, takes a good cut, sands well and finishes nicely. More experienced carvers may want to choose a harder wood from the chart on page 16.

For the patterns in this book, choose a piece of basswood 4" wide by 11" long (102mm x 279mm) and 1/2" to 1 1/2" thick. Some patterns may take less. The thickness of your wood will determine the depth of the spoon bowl or accommodate a curved-handle design.

The hardness and texture of the piece of wood you choose will vary depending on where the tree was grown and the climate in that area. You will have these "special features" to deal with in almost any wood you choose. Don't become discouraged if you get a difficult piece of wood. Try again. You will develop preferences for certain woods based on your own carving style, choice of pattern, available tools and carving technique.

Spoon carving requires so little wood that a scrap to a woodworker or furniture maker could be the beginnings of a beautiful masterpiece for a spoon carver. An old log or trimmings from your neighbor's tree

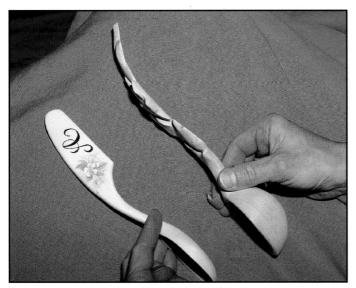

There are a few patterns with curved or offset handles. Your wood thickness will need to accommodate not only the depth of the spoon bowl, but also the curve of the handle.

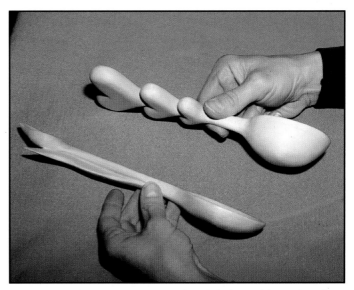

The spoon at the top was cut from 1 1/2-inch-thick wood (38mm). The spoon at the bottom was cut from 3/4-inch-thick material (19mm). You can see how the thickness of the wood can determine a spoon's bowl shape.

shouldn't be overlooked. The only "rule" in selecting wood for spoon carving applies if you are carving spoons to be used with food. If this is the case, choose a strong, close-grained, non-resinous, unscented, non-spalted wood such as cherry or maple. (Food safe finishes will be covered later in this chapter.)

Below is a table of suggested spoon-carving woods and their characteristics. Think of it only as a beginning and add to your repertoire of wood experiences as often as you can.

Some wood species are rare and their source forests are threatened with extinction. I urge all woodcarvers and woodworkers to be responsible when choosing and using wood.

Patterns

Patterns for spoons often show only the front of the spoon. Side-view patterns are needed only if the handle of a spoon is curved.

To transfer patterns to the wood, you can use any one of a number of methods. I commonly use carbon paper slipped carbon-side down between the pattern and the wood. Tracing over the pattern lines with a pencil or other pointed object will leave an outline on the wood. In the absence of carbon paper, you can use a lead pencil to "color" on the back of a pattern. This creates a make-shift carbon paper and the pattern lines will appear on the wood when traced over. You can also make a photocopy of the pattern, place it black-side down on the wood, and use a hot iron to transfer the lines to the wood. There are countless other ways to transfer patterns. A bit of experimentation will show you which way works best for you.

Wood	Botanical Name	Hardness	Color	Grain	Use with Food
Fruitwoods	various	hard	various	various	
Basswood	Tilia americana	soft	very light	straight, fine	yes
Butternut	Juglans cinerea	medium	medium brown	straight, coarse	
Catalpa	Catalpa speciosa	soft	medium brown	coarse	
Aromatic Cedar	Juniperus virginiana	medium	light to red	straight, fine	no
Cherry	Prunus serotina	hard	light red	straight, fine	yes
Maple	Umbellularia californica	hard	light	straight, fine	yes
Oak	Quercus spp.	hard	light	variable, coarse	yes
Walnut	Juglans nigra	hard	dark	variable, coarse	yes
Willow	Salix spp.	medium	light	straight, fine	
Cottonwood, Poplar, Aspen	Populus spp.	medium	light	straight fine	
Mahogany	Swietenia macrophylla	medium-hard	red	straight coarse	
Pine, white	Pinus strobus	soft	light	straight	no

Bowl and Handle Designs

Beginners will most likely want to try their hand at carving spoons from the patterns in this book. I picked spoon designs with different bowl shapes to give you a wide variety from which to choose. Make sure that as a beginner, you choose an appropriate pattern for your first project. Choosing a pattern that is too difficult may cause you to become frustrated. It's best to start small and then build up to those more intricate patterns.

After you've carved several spoons, you may even want to think about creating your own spoon designs. The best way to start is to make new combinations of the design elements found in the spoon patterns in this book. Simply mix and match handle patterns with bowl patterns. I have included many different bowl shapes to give you a variety from which to choose in the pattern section.

To mix and match, first trace the handle. Then move your tracing over the bowl patterns until you find one you like. Trace the bowl. Make sure the transition from the bowl to the handle is smooth, pleasing to the eye and not too thin or weak.

You can lengthen or shorten the handles by moving your tracing as necessary, copying the parts of the pattern you need. A good place on the pattern to lengthen the handle is just above where the bowl meets the handle. Longer handles are perfect for items such as salad serving utensils.

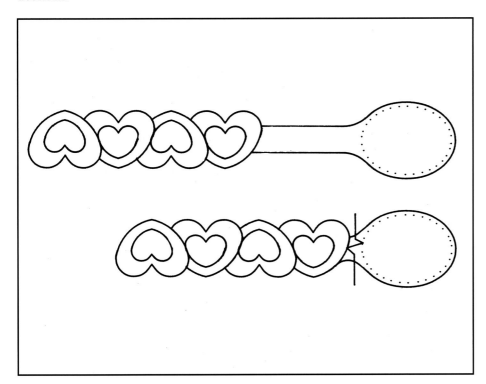

Make longer handles for salad utensils by lengthening the spoon handles just above the bowl.

You may make any of the spoon designs into a fork design by removing a semi-circular or semi-elliptical piece. If you are making a salad serving set, make the bowl depth quite shallow and the spoon bowl fairly large in diameter.

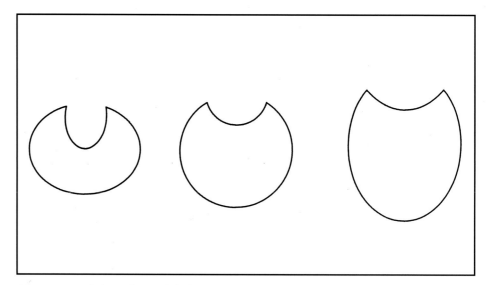

Spoons can easily be made into forks by removing semi-circular or semi-elliptical shapes to alter the bowl.

Any of the handle designs can be easily adapted to create a letter opener. Just remove the spoon bowl and add the shape shown below or one of your own design. Carve, shape and sand the "blade" until it can be used as an effective letter-opening tool. The letter opener should be carved from one of the harder woods like walnut or cherry.

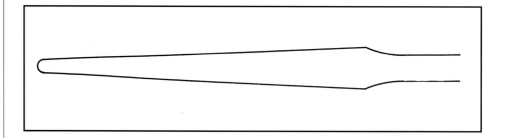

Making Curved Handles

Any of the handle patterns can be made into a curved handle. The thickness of your wood will determine how curved you can make the handle. The thicker the wood, the more curved your handle will be.

You can cut a curved handle one of two ways. The first way is to cut out the outline on a bandsaw and then carve away all of the waste wood until you get the handle shape you want. The second way is to cut out the outline, then turn the spoon 90 degrees and cut out the curved handle. The steps that make this easy are shown below.

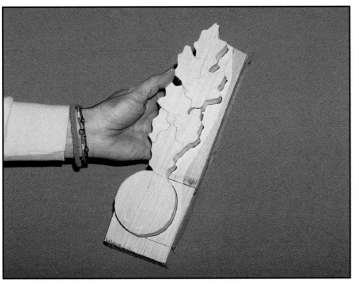

Cut out the outline of the spoon.

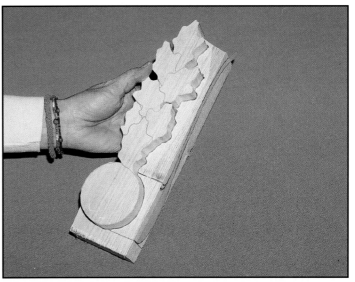

Save the waste wood from one side of your cut out. Draw a line from the intersection of the bowl to handle across the top of this waste piece and down the side. Now you will know where to position your side view.

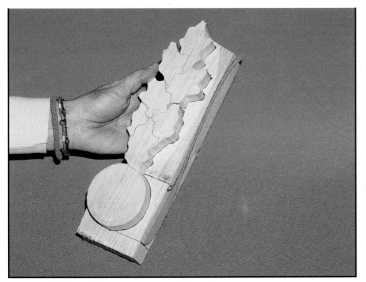

Draw the side view on, or glue the traced side view onto the wood.

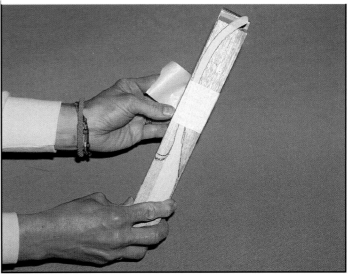

Tape the waste piece and the spoon cutout together. Now you can cut the curved handle pattern on your band saw.

Ladles

With a thick enough piece of wood you can angle the spoon bowl to make your spoon more ladle-shaped. The strength of the transition from bowl to handle will diminish a bit if you rotate the bowl up from the grain direction. If you want to carve a ladle, use hardwood.

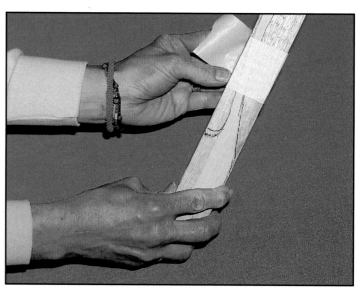

Make a spoon into a ladle by angling the spoon bowl.

Leftovers

For each spoon you carve, you will have the left-over waste wood from the handle. If you are a metal worker (or know one), you might make a metal letter-opener blade and insert it into this waste piece of wood. Carve the handle and you will have a nice letter opener.

Metal blades can be added to left-over wood to make letter openers.

Making a Model

Some patterns get a bit complicated. Handle designs featuring entwined rope can be very intricate. These are not hard to carve, but they are hard to picture in your mind. When this is the case, I often make a rope model to help me envision a project and to act as a guide. You may find that models of cardboard or modeling clay will help you with other patterns. Below is an example of how to make a rope model.

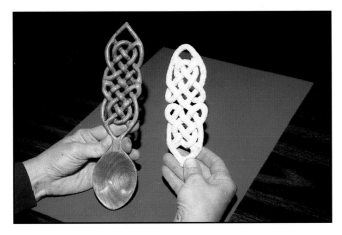

1. Here is an example of one of those hard-to-envision designs, so I made a rope model to have something to look at while I carve.

2. As you can see, a side view drawing would not have helped much.

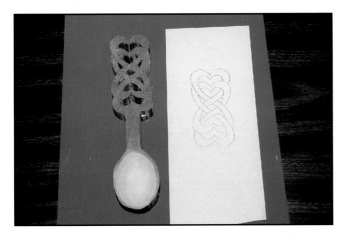

3. Now lets go over the steps for making a model for this spoon. As you can see, I've carved and sanded the bowl but I need a little help on the handle to visualize how the hearts intertwine. First trace the handle portion of the spoon.

4. I have a small (approximately 8 inch by 8 inch) piece of scrap wood on which I've glued two ⅛" layers of cork. This will be my work surface.

5. Tape the pattern over the cork and cover with plastic wrap or waxed paper.

6. I use cotton rope about ¼ inch in diameter and cut a bit longer than I need for the pattern.

7. Put the rope into a plastic bag with fabric stiffener (available from fabric or sewing stores) or white glue.

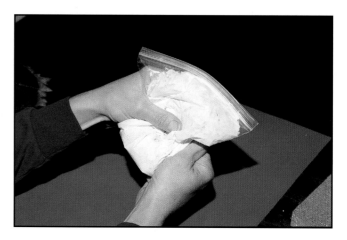

8. Knead until the rope is completely coated with glue or stiffener.

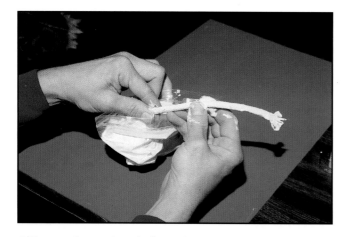

9. Remove the rope from the bag and wipe off the excess glue.

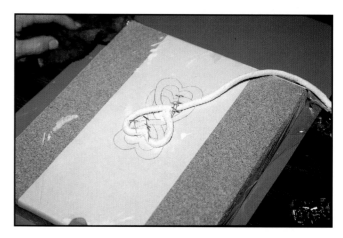

10. Now pin the rope over the pattern. I use "T" pins because they are easier to handle.

11. Keep working.

12. Be sure to model the over-under pattern correctly.

13. One last check of the model.

14. Looks good. Now put it aside to dry for 24 hours.

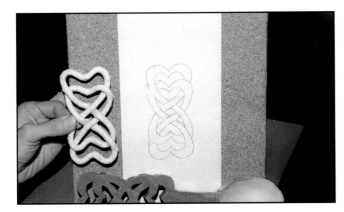

15. Here is the finished model, pattern and spoon. Ready for carving. Just a hint about how to start the woven spoon handles. Don't carve the overlapping ropes apart, leave them together for strength. They will take on the appearance of being separate as you carve and sand. You can take it from here. The Gallery has pictures of some of the finished woven spoons.

Sanding Tips

I sand my spoons beginning with about 80-grit sandpaper, going to 100 or 120 and then to 220 and finer depending on the wood, the design I have chosen and the finish I want. Synthetic abrasive pads are also available in various grades. You can cut these to shape to make them easier to use. Even a brown paper bag will make a good final finish cloth.

Between grades of sandpaper, be sure to brush off your wood piece. If you leave old abrasive grit, it will cut grooves as you continue sanding with the finer paper. A soft paint brush or a soft toothbrush works well for removing grit.

A tip for those who plan to make chip-carved spoons: Do all sanding before you chip carve. Sanding after chip carving will round the edges of your design. You want them crisp and clean.

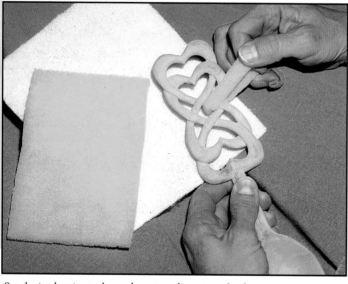

Synthetic abrasive pads can be cut to shape to make them easier to use for sanding spoons.

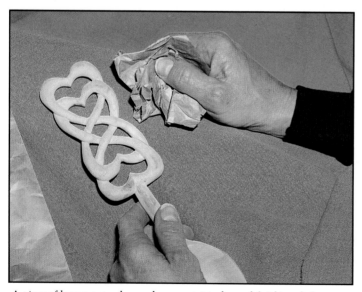

A piece of brown paper bag makes a surprisingly good finishing cloth.

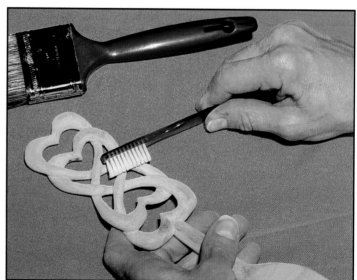

Between sandings, use a soft paint brush or toothbrush to gently remove any grit left by the sandpaper.

Spoon Carving Basics   Carving Your First Spoon   Carving the Welsh Love Spoon   Patterns

24

Carving Spoons

Finishing Tips

Let the design of your carving dictate the finish. For ornamental spoons, two coats of a good polyurethane finish will be adequate to protect the wood and enhance the design. You can choose from a matte, semi-gloss or gloss finish. Remember when you're choosing a finish to keep the design of your spoon in mind. A glossy finish will reflect more light and make the deep areas of your carving appear less defined. For this reason, it is better to choose a matte finish for more intricate designs. Glossy finishes are good for simpler patterns.

Polyurethane may foam as you apply it. Don't leave these bubbles on your carving because they will leave marks in an otherwise smooth finish. Use a dry rag to remove some of the polyurethane from your brush, then, using your "dry" brush, "paint" your carving until the bubbles are gone. Also, don't allow any finish to pool in deep areas of your carving. Excess finish in these areas will make them appear shallow and uninteresting. Use the dry brush technique described above to remove excess polyurethane from the crevasses of your work.

Drying times for polyurethane finishes vary depending on the humidity and temperature of the air and the thickness of the coat. Test your finish by pushing your thumbnail into the finish. If your nail leaves a mark, allow some extra drying time. After the first coat of polyurethane finish is dry, you can sand the piece lightly with a very fine sandpaper, fine emery cloth or 4x0 steel wool. Remove the sanding residue with a soft brush or tack cloth, then apply the second coat. Repeat the sanding step before all additional coats of polyurethane.

For chip carving or highly detailed relief carving you will need a thinner finish so that it will not build up or pool in the detail of the carved piece. A spray polyurethane or a thinned polyurethane applied with a brush are good finishes for these carving styles. A satin or semi-gloss is best; a very glossy finish will reflect too much light not allowing the shadows to emphasize the depth and detail of your work.

You may choose to oil your finished piece with linseed oil. Linseed oil will give a very flat finish and is good for intricate designs. Apply linseed oil with a soft rag, wipe off the excess and allow the spoon to dry. Apply a second coat in the same manner. There is one pattern in this book that definitely calls for an oil finish. The spoon with the carved chain and the ball in the cage should not be finished with polyurethane. Polyurethane will cause the chains to stick together and keep the ball from moving freely in the cage. Use tung or linseed oil and follow the directions on the can.

Food Safe Finishes

Spoons being used to serve food require special non-toxic finishes and special care during use to make them serviceable and keep them clean. Neglecting to finish and care for your carved spoons will result in their shortened life. With proper care they will certainly become heirlooms.

Do not use salad or cooking oil as a wood preservative as these can become stale or rancid. A thin coating of mineral oil is a good option. There are some permanent salad bowl finishes that are not toxic after they cure. Read and follow all of the instructions for preparing and finishing the wood if you choose this type of product.

Care recommended for a good wooden salad bowl, cutting board or butcher block will be adequate for your spoons. Wash your woodenware by hand with a mild dish soap and warm water. Do not allow your woodenware to soak for any period of time in water. Dry your spoon immediately with a soft cloth. Additional air drying for a few hours is fine. If you have not used a permanent salad bowl finish, coat your spoons with a food safe wood preserver such as mineral oil before you store them. Do not carve intricate designs in the bowls of spoons used to serve food. These bowls should be left plain and smooth so food will not be trapped.

Common Mistakes and How to Fix Them

If you continue to carve spoons, eventually you will make a mistake that appears disastrous at first. Don't be discouraged. Here are a couple of "solutions" to try before deciding to throw your work into the scrap pile.

One common mistake is to carve a bowl too deep and end up cutting a hole through the bottom or side of the bowl. To correct this mistake, shape the hole like a heart, leaf or scroll. You may need to intentionally

An accidental hole punched in a spoon bowl can be corrected by carving it into a heart, leaf or scroll shape.

Carving Spoons

add other holes to balance your new "design." Sandpaper the edges of the holes to smooth and round them. It will be beautiful....just like you planned it.

Too much pressure or not enough wood can make a spoon break during carving. What a terrible feeling to be carving one piece of wood and suddenly end up with two or more pieces in your hand! Take a deep breath, relax and get a bottle of glue. I use white, clear-drying craft glue, but you will want to use waterproof wood glue if you intend to use a water-based finish or if you will be washing your spoon. Test fit the broken piece before you apply the glue. Get a good feeling for the way the wood grain of the broken pieces fits back together. And remember not to sand or carve or make any adjustments to your carving until you've glued the broken piece and it has dried thoroughly. If you make a good glue joint, you won't be able to find it when your carving is sanded and finished.

Chapter Two
Carving Your First Spoon

This first carving project is truly organized and presented for someone who has never carved before. I have made the steps quite detailed to build your confidence as you go. If you are a more advanced carver with your own techniques, skip to the patterns in the back, pick one and just have fun!

The pattern I'm using for this demonstration was used to make the first spoon I carved. The pattern is from Van Dowda, my uncle and best carving buddy. I carved this spoon and just couldn't stop. I hope you enjoy it, too.

NOTE: If the spoons shown in this book are flat-handled spoons, they will not have a side-view pattern. For most spoons, a side view does not better explain the design. A side view of a bowl might indicate only one wood thickness, when in fact, any thickness from $1/2$" up to $1\ 1/2$" inch will do nicely. Side-view patterns for the spoons in this book are included only for spoons with curved handles or where a side view will aid the carver. The spoon I'm carving in this demonstration is a flat-handled spoon. The pattern is found on page 53.

The thickness of wood you choose can be anywhere from $1/2$" to $1\ 1/2$" thick. If this is your first spoon, a piece from $3/4$" thick to 1" thick would be good (13 to 19mm). The wood should measure at least 4" wide by 11" long with the grain running along the length of the wood. Basswood is a good wood for beginning carvers. More advanced carvers may want to choose a wood from the chart on page 16.

Transfer the pattern to your wood and cut out using a band saw, scroll saw, or jig saw.

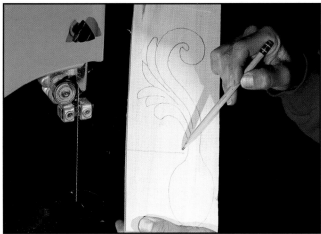

I've trimmed my board a bit so it is easier to handle. Draw a line on the board at the point of the spoon where the bowl transitions into the handle.

Continue this transition line over onto the side of the board. Then draw a vertical line to meet it. This vertical line will represent the thickness of the spoon handle.

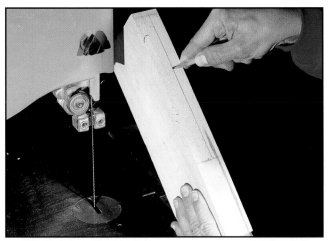

For this spoon we will use approximately $1/2''$ or around 13mm for the handle thickness.

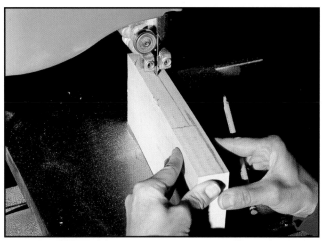

On the bandsaw, cut the handle thickness line.

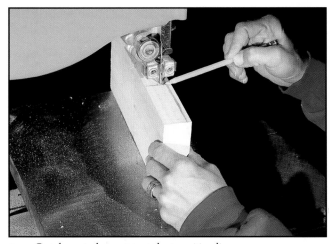

Cut down to but not past the transition line.

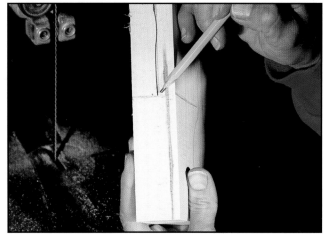

Stop your cut right there and back the blade out of the wood. Don't worry if this cut is not perfect. If it is plus or minus $1/8''$ it will be fine. Do not remove the waste handle wood. This wood will give strength to the handle and give you something to grip while you carve the spoon bowl.

Bowl Depth

Carving the depth of the spoon bowl can be tricky. One method to help you gage the depth of the bowl is shown below. For your first spoon, we will leave the bottom of the spoon bowl about 1/4" thick and the sides about 1/8" to 3/16" thick. The other method is just to carve by feel. Carve the bowl slowly and when you think you are close to the desired depth, use your thumb on the bottom of the spoon and your finger on the inside of the bowl to feel and measure the depth. This is easy and will come quite naturally after you have carved one or two spoons.

1. Chuck a drill bit (about 1/8" diameter) in your hand drill or drill press. Gage the bit so that you drill a hole leaving about 1/4" of wood at the center of the spoon bowl.

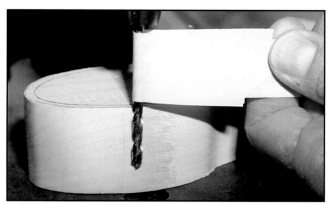

2. Wrap tape around the bit to act as a "stop" indicator.

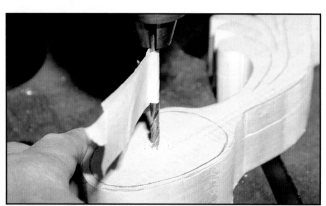

3. Drill the hole in the center of the spoon bowl or at the point that will be the deepest part of the bowl. Stop when the tape touches the top of your board. When you carve the bowl to the depth of this hole, then you know to stop. The 1/4" will give you enough wood to shape and sand both the inside and outside of the spoon bowl.

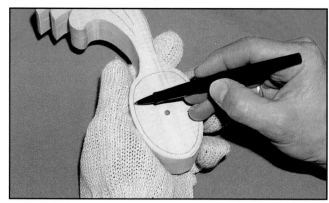

4. Now you are almost ready to start carving. You should draw a line 1/8" to 3/16" inside the outer bowl line of your pattern. (Most of the patterns have this dashed line.) We will call this the inner wall line. If you enlarge or reduce patterns, remember to redraw this inner line to leave 1/8" or a bit more to create the wall thickness for the spoon bowl.

Carving the Bowl

Keep in mind that you don't have to complete this carving in one day. In fact, you may only want to carve for fifteen minutes. If your hands or eyes get tired, stop, put your carving down, get up and walk around. Injuries and mistakes often occur when you are tired.

Get out your glove, sharp tools and pattern before you start. We talked about grain direction before and this is the place where this concept will become most obvious.

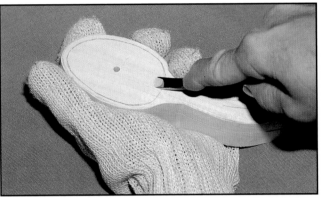

5. Begin by holding the bowl of your spoon with the handle toward you. Start at the top (handle side) of the bowl on the inside wall line. Insert your spoon gouge about ¹/₃₂" or about .5mm. Push in the gouge and at the same time gently and slowly push down on the handle.

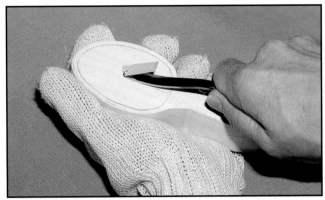

6. This will cut the wood and lift the blade of the gouge out of the wood so you will be ready for the next cut. This is the same motion you would use if you were trying to spoon very hard ice cream. If your tools are sharp, it should feel about the same.

7. Carving in one direction will produce a smooth curl of wood. This is "with the grain."

8. Carving in the other direction will produce a rough, unpredictable splinter of wood. This is "against the grain." Don't worry about visually analyzing grain direction. If you start to carve and discover you are getting an unpredictable splintering chip, you are going against the grain. Just turn your work around. On the bowl, you will be forced to carve part of it against the grain. Always start your gouge cut on the internal wall line and work to the center. If there is any tearout it will be in the area you are going to remove.

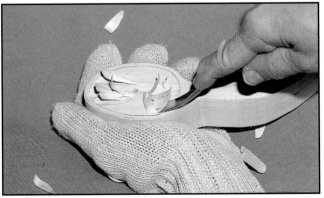

9. Take only very small "bites" as you continue this process around the line. Don't push the gouge all the way to the center because these first few cuts will want to tear all the way across the bowl.

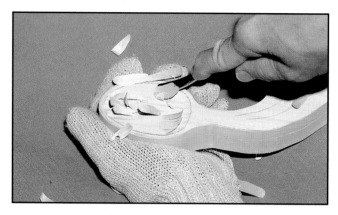

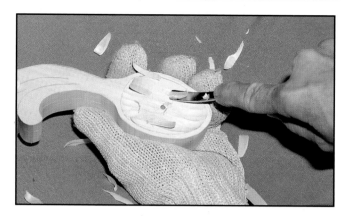

10. You will not work across the grain as you go around, but always with the grain, using short strokes as you work on the sides of the bowl.

11. Keep going. Photos 11-15 show how wood is removed from the bowl.

12.

13.

14.

15.

16. You can still see the depth drill hole, but the next few cuts will remove it.

17. Looks good. I think this is fine.

18. Now sand the inside of the spoon bowl with the 80-grit sandpaper.

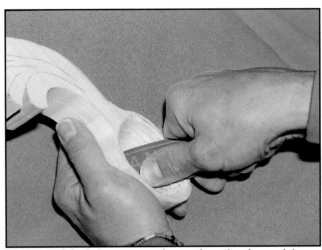

19. We sand this before we carve the outside so if we have a deformation or thin place we can compensate for it with the outside wall.

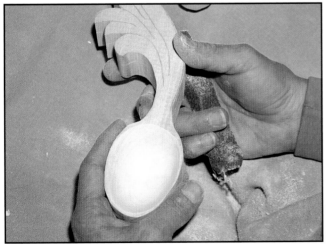

20. Your first sanding for the bowl inside is finished.

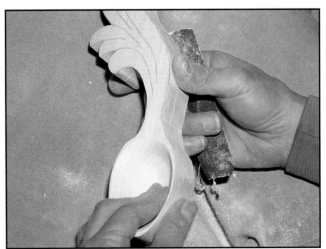

21. Your fingers can feel very small deformations in a surface. Use your fingers to check the shape of your spoon bowl. Close your eyes. Your eye can be fooled by the wood grain, but not your fingertips. Clean up any problems before moving on to the outside of the spoon bowl.

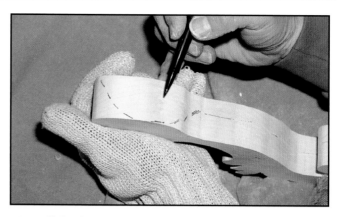

22. Now on to the outside of the spoon bowl. Make a pencil mark on the bottom of the spoon at the lowest point of the bowl. This will be the place where you leave the most material. You will not carve this line away, but will carve up to it and sand it away when you refine the finished shape of the spoon bowl outside.

23. I will sketch an idea for the spoon bowl outside so you can see what our goal is here. Don't depend on a line for your carving. Just try to match the inside bowl shape with the outside wall. Do this by eye and by feel.

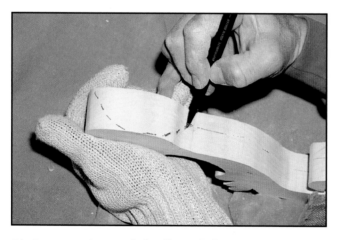

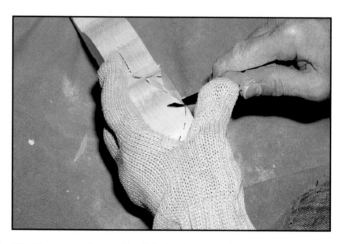

24. A transition line into the handle may be helpful.

25. Now carve the outside of the bowl using a slicing cut. Carve so that the outside parallels the inside contour that you've just sanded. Leave the wall thickness $1/8''$ (3mm) to $3/16''$ (4.5mm) thick. I have some spoon bowls that are thicker and they look fine too.

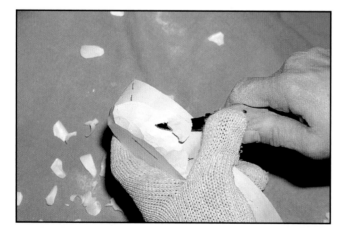

26. You will find that your bowl outside carves nicely one direction but produces torn chips the other way. The point on the spoon bowl where this change takes place is at the middle or in most cases, the widest part of the spoon bowl. This is the effect of grain direction again, combined with the shape of the bowl.

27. Just turn your work around and carve the other way.

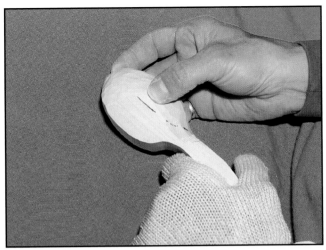

28. *Again, use your finger and thumb to gage the shape and thickness of the spoon bowl. Now carve the other side.*

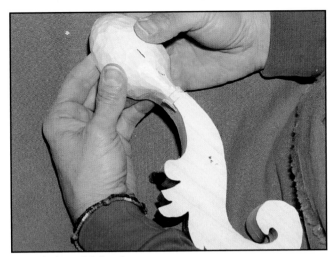

29. *It looks and feels right.*

30. *Look for symmetry or a pleasing shape to your spoon bowl. Make any adjustments you think are necessary.*

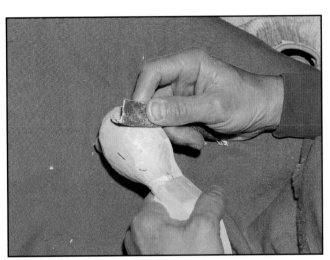

31. *Now sand the outside of the bowl with 80 grit.*

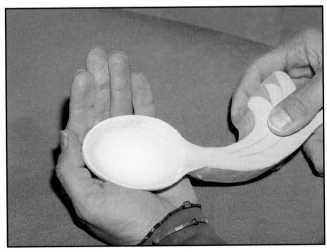

32. *Round over the edge of the spoon bowl with your sandpaper and again look for symmetry.*

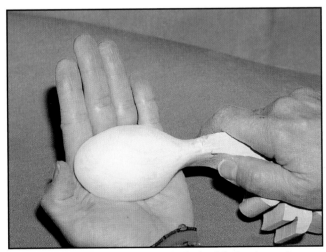

33. *Turn the spoon over and check the back of the bowl as well.*

Carving the Handle

Now you are ready to carve the handle. There are only two cuts we will use for carving any of the spoon handles: a stop cut and a slicing cut. It is that simple. A stop cut just outlines the area you are working on and prevents the wood from tearing across this line. The slicing cut removes the wood up to the stop cut or shapes from high areas to low areas. That's really all there is to it.

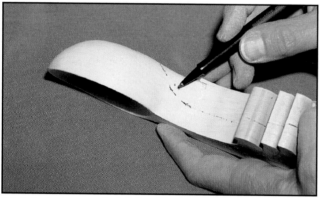

34. *It is time to start the handle. This line is the transition line from the bowl to the handle. Remove the waste handle wood by carving the transition from the bowl to the handle.*

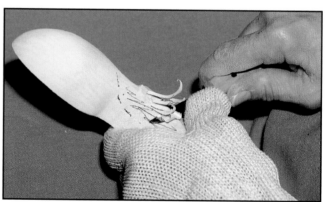

35. *Remove wood from this area of the handle in small slivers. Use the knife to carefully remove the waste wood.*

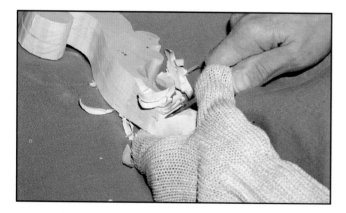

36. *Turn the spoon around and continue making shallow cuts to remove the wood.*

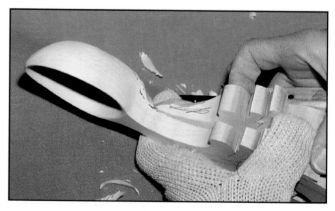

37. *As the wood is removed the waste wood on the handle starts to break away.*

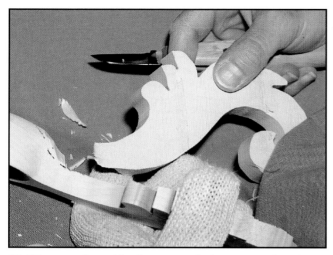

38. When enough wood has been removed, the waste wood on the handle can be removed.

39. You want a smooth transition that leaves a radius or web of material here to give strength to the handle.

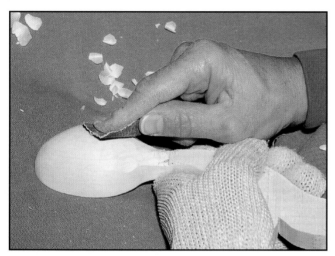

40. With the 80 grit, smooth the transition area.

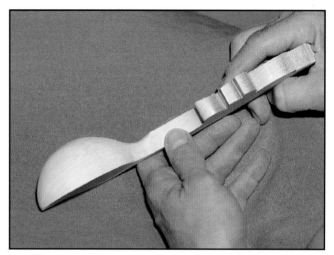

41. Look at it from different directions. Are you pleased? If not make any adjustments you need by additional carving or sanding. If you must carve more, remember to clean off all of the sanding grit before you use your knife or the grit will dull the blade.

42. Look at your spoon handle. We will begin by carving the left most leaf. This leaf is peaked in the middle and drops away on both sides. Therefore the peak will be the closest to you and will be the area of least material removed. The edges of the leaf will be the areas where you remove the most material. Work from the top of the spoon to the center of the handle thickness for now. We will work from the back later.

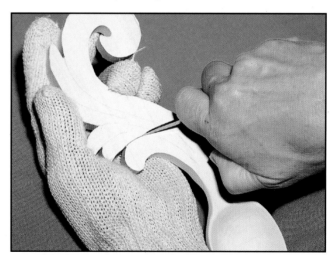

43. Outline your leaf with a stop cut. This cut is perpendicular to the surface of your wood.

44. *Slice up to the stop cut to create depth and define this leaf. Repeat the stop cut and slice cuts until you get the leaf shaped on the inside.*

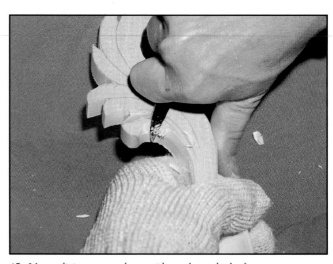

45. *Use a slicing cut on the outside to shape the leaf.*

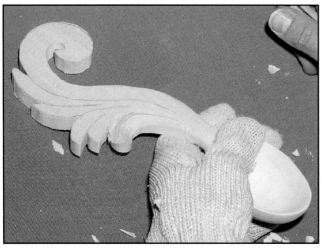

46. *This leaf is complete on the front side. We have taken the shaping process to the center on the thickness of the handle.*

47. *We will continue the shaping from the back. You may choose not to carve the backs of your spoons. If this is your choice, take the shaping of the edges of the design from the front to the full thickness of the wood and round over the back edges a bit. Be sure to sand the back smooth.*

48. *Keep in mind that whatever was most visible on the top side may be covered on the back. If you need help visualizing this, cut the leaf shapes out of paper and glue them together as you want them to be in your carving. Then look at the front and the back.*

49. *The second leaf is behind the first and third leaves.*

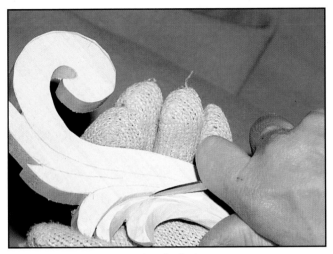

50. Make the stop cuts to outline this leaf.

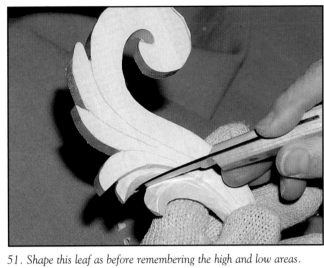

51. Shape this leaf as before remembering the high and low areas. Just carve the top, we will get to the back later.

52. Go on to the next leaf on the top side.

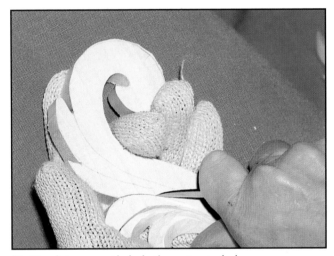

53. Use slicing cuts with the knife to separate the leaves.

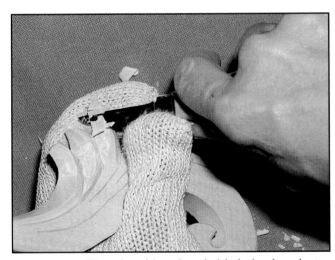

54. Remove small bits of wood from the end of the leaf to shape the tip.

55. Skip to the large leaf - the most dominant one. Use the stop cut to outline and the slicing cut to shape.

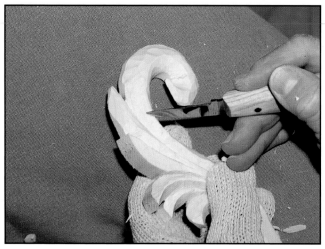

56. Peak the center of this leaf.

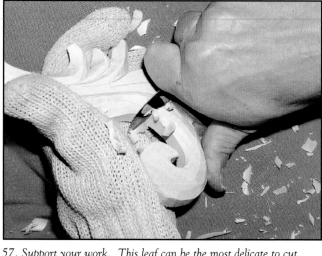

57. Support your work. This leaf can be the most delicate to cut.

58. Work on the remaining two leaves in the same manner.

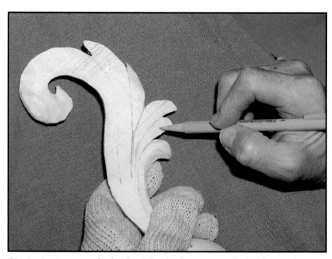

59. Let's return to the back. This leaf was partially hidden in the front view, so more of it will be visible in the back view.

60. Keep that in mind as your carve the back of the spoon.

61. You can create some interest and movement in the leaves by carving their tips bending front to back.

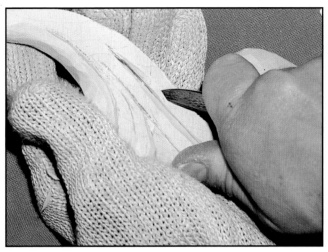

62. Detailing the back of a spoon is not always necessary depending on how your finished spoon will be displayed or used.

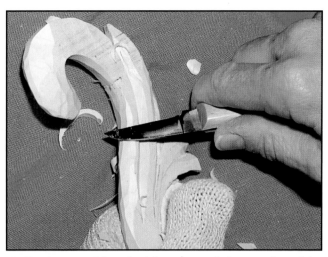

63. For this spoon, I have decided to separate the leaves and round the edges on the back side of the spoon. Nicely formed leaves will give the spoon a more finished look when the spoon is viewed from the side.

64. The back of the handle is now finished

65. Turn the spoon over and check the leaves from the front.

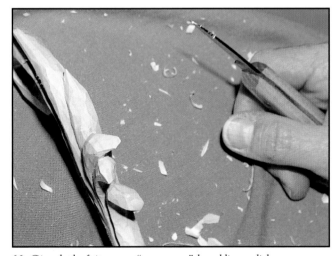

66. Give the leaf tips some "movement" by adding a slight curve to the ends.

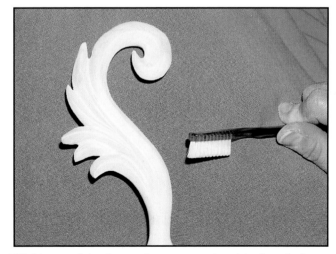

67. Use a tooth brush to gently remove wood particles from the front of the finished spoon. Turn the spoon over and brush the back as well.

Sanding and Finishing

Before you start to sand and finish, make sure you are happy with your spoon the way it is. Check it over one last time for imperfections. Close your eyes and feel the bowl with your fingers. Is it as even and as smooth as you can make it? Open your eyes and look closely at the spoon handle. Are there any parts of the design that need to be touched up?

When you are happy with what you have, sand the spoon first with 80-grit sandpaper, then use finer grits until you are happy with the finished spoon. Remember to brush away the grit between sanding steps and also after final sanding.

68. *Because this spoon is for decorative purposes only, we'll use polyurethane to finish it. Paint on a coat of polyurethane. I used gloss. Your polyurethane may foam. Don't let these bubbles stay on your piece. "Paint" your brush on a dry rag to remove some of the polyurethane. Then go over your spoon with this dry brush to even the coat of poly and remove the bubbles or any finish that has pooled in low places.*

69. *Hang your spoon to dry.*

70. *After the poly dries, sand your spoon with very fine sandpaper (400 or better), fine emery cloth or 4x0 steel wool. Remove the residue from this process with a tack cloth and then paint a second coat. Repeat this step for each coat of polyurethane you wish to apply.*

Chapter Three
Carving the Welsh Love Spoon

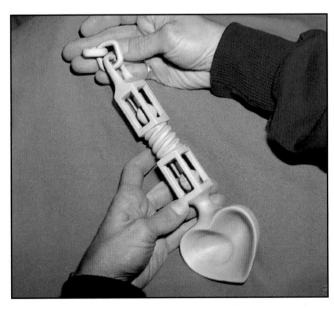

1. This spoon was adapted from an old Welsh design. You may make the chain as long as your wood allows, just continue to trace the links until you get the number you want.

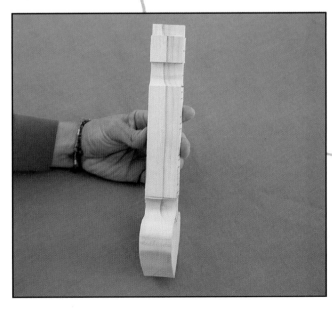

2. The handle design is square, so you need at least 1 1/4" (31.75mm) thick wood. I used 1 1/2" thick wood because that is what I had on hand. Cut out the design.

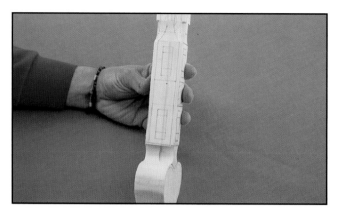

3. I glued a tissue paper pattern centered on the side, so I would know where to cut.

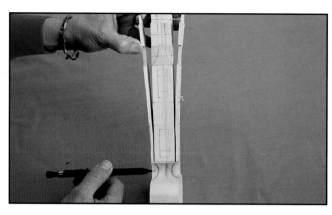

4. Cut away the excess thickness (if you have any) from both the front and back of the handle to keep your design centered. Note the transition from bowl to handle that I have sketched on.

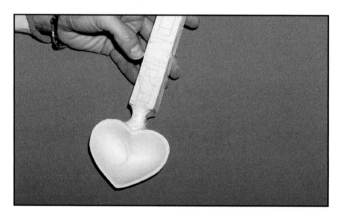

5. Carve the inside of the spoon bowl with a gouge and the outside of the spoon bowl with a knife. Use your fingers to check for imperfections in the spoon wall.

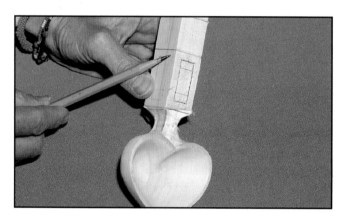

6. We need to draw the design on all four sides of the handle. Make sure that the lines of the cage continue correctly around the handle. Take time to do this precisely. It will make carving easier.

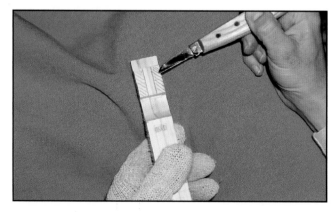

7. We begin by carving the chain. Look at the pattern drawing and finished spoon. Make marks with a pencil to indicate the areas you want to remove.

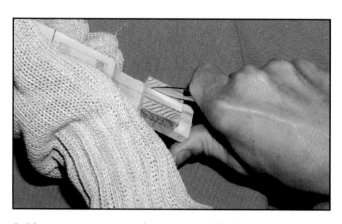

8. Now use your two cuts, the stop cut and the slicing cut, to remove the waste wood. First stop cut perpendicular to the surface of the wood.

9. Slice cut to remove material up to the stop cut.

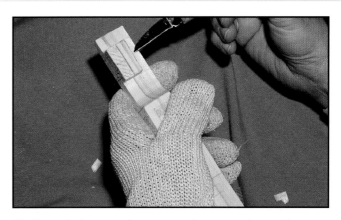

10. Repeat both cuts until you remove the unwanted material.

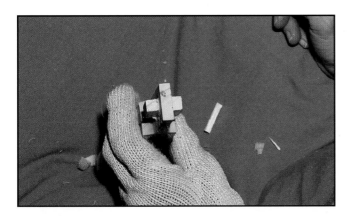

11. When you've finished this step all around, the end of the spoon handle will look like this.

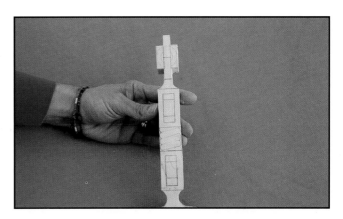

12. With the bowl of your spoon facing you, you will see two chain links with the narrow part facing you and one link turned the other way.

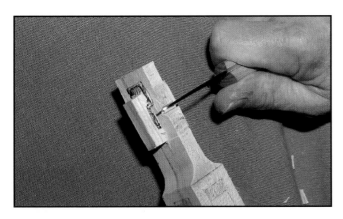

13. We begin separating the two links with a v-cut. (Stop cuts in a "V" shape).

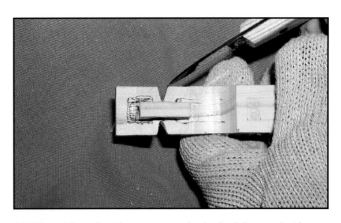

14. Viewed from the side you can see the depth of the completed v-cuts.

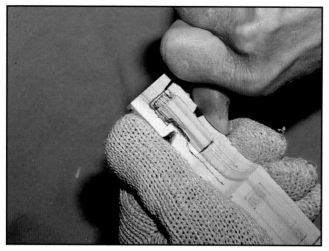

15. On all the links, color in the area of waste wood that you want to remove.

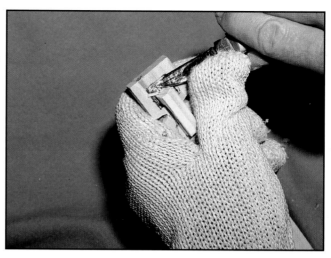

16. Carefully remove the waste wood with slow, controlled cuts.

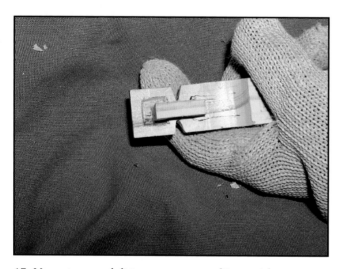

17. Use stop cuts and slicing cuts to remove this material.

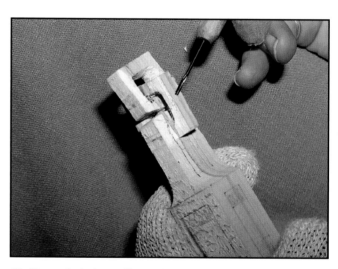

18. You might find a small gouge helpful to separate the links.

19. One link is free. Round and smooth.

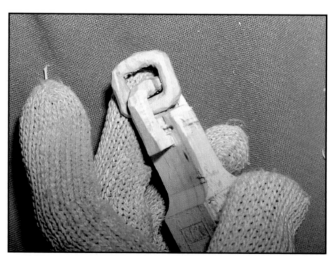

20. After the link has been rounded it will turn freely on the end of the spoon.

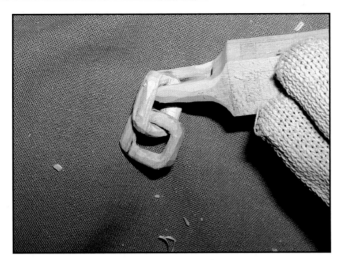

21. Complete the rest of the chain links in the same manner.

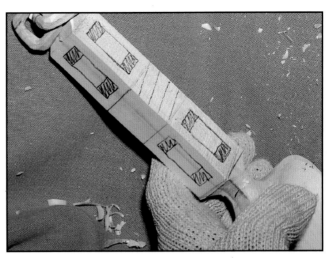

22. Now on to the ball in the cage. Your design should be drawn on all four sides of the handle and the wood you want to remove should be marked.

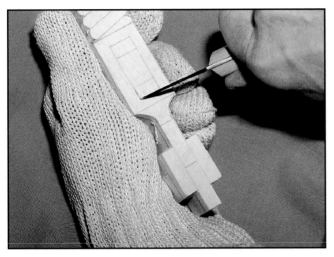

23. Stop cut. It is very important that your stop cuts for the cage are perpendicular to the surface of the wood.

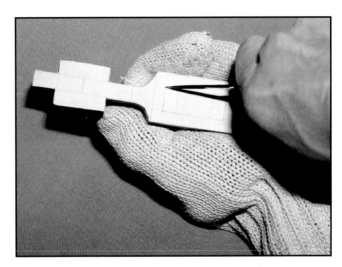

24. Perpendicular cuts are necessary to keep the cage bars even and straight.

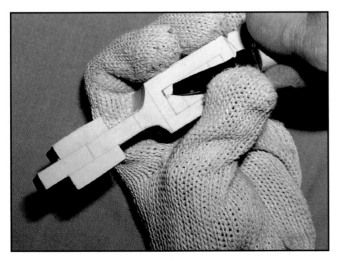

25. Slice cut to remove waste wood.

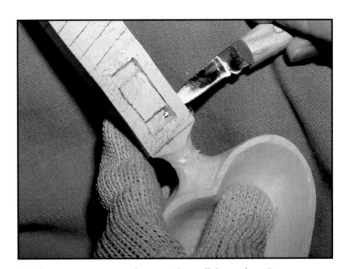

26. Continue to remove the waste from all four sides. Soon your knife blade will show through.

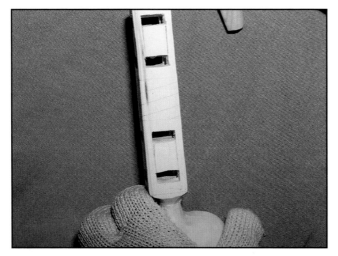

27. All waste removed. The remaining wood will become the ball. If you are still wondering how the ball stays in the cage, look at the pattern drawing for the cross section view.

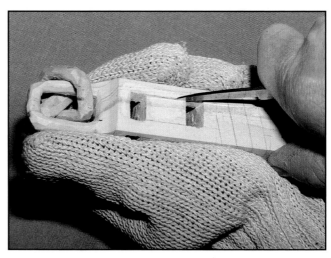

28. You must "free" this shape from the bars of the cage with stop and slicing cuts. Again, be sure to maintain the perpendicularity of the stop cuts to the surface of the cage side you are working on.

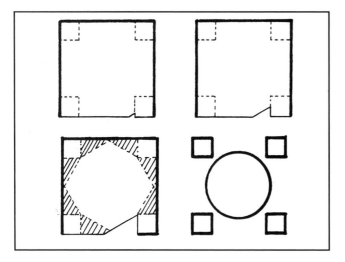

29. This illustration shows the series of slicing cuts that will free the plug.

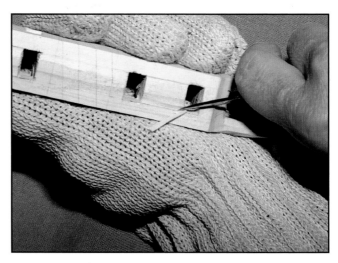

30. Just before you make the break through cuts, begin to round the ball. It is easier to do the rounding while the ball is still captive.

31. The ball is free.

32. Continue rounding to a ball shape.

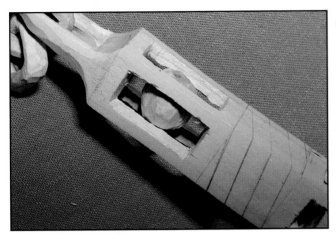

33. *The ball freely rolls in the cage.*

34. *Now let's carve the center spiral. You must draw this design all the way around your handle, continuing the line of the spiral as you go. Here is an easy way to do this. Take a thick piece of paper or card stock. Lay the straight edge along the spiral line from the front view on your spoon or on the pattern. Mark the points where the vertical edge of the handle meets the card.*

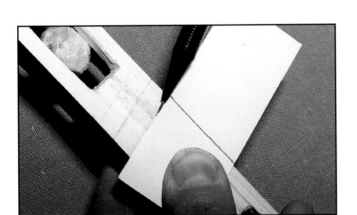

35. *Draw a line to connect those points. Now if you line up the line you just drew on the straight edge of the handle and place the top of the line at the point where the spiral from the front surface meets the corner, you can continue the spiral on around the handle at the same angle.*

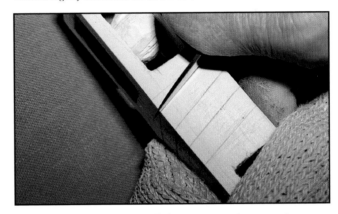

36. *Begin carving the spiral with the stop cut on the pattern line.*

37. *Cut into the stop cut with the slicing cut to round and smooth the spiral all the way around the handle.*

38. *You will be removing the most material on the corners to make this section round.*

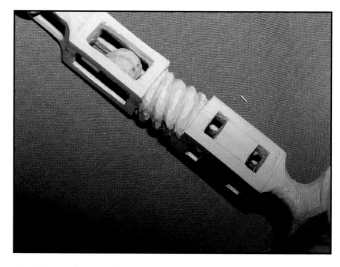

39. The spiral is complete.

Sanded and finished spoon front and back. Use an oil finish such as tung or linseed oil for this spoon. Follow the directions on the can.

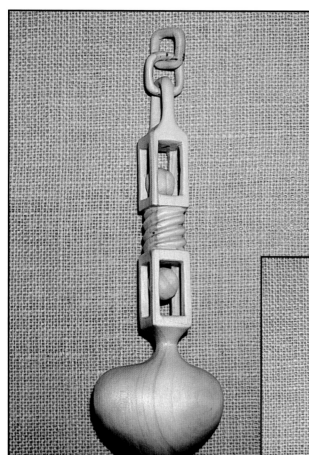

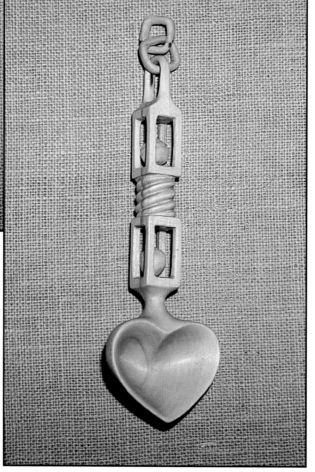

Chapter Four
Gallery

Here are photos of some of the spoon patterns that have been carved. All of the spoons pictured in the gallery have corresponding patterns in the next chapter. Remember that this is only one interpretation of the design. You may choose to carve yours in a different way.

The painting on the handle of the left-most spoon was done with watercolor pencils on the sanded but unfinished basswood. The second spoon from the right is the Welsh love spoon carved in chapter three. The remaining spoons are chip-carved by Van Dowda.

More intricate designs, such as those pictured on the spoon handles here, may be difficult to envision. A model made from string will help you understand overlapping designs. The leaf spoon in the bottom left corner will be a "family tree" spoon. I intend to add names of family members— one for each leaf – in gold paint.

Bowl shapes can be any size and depth. Oftentimes, the shape of the bowl will be chosen to balance the design of the spoon handle. The heart carved in the bowl of the spoon on the bottom right is a nice ornamental effect. It can also be used to hide a hole punched through a spoon bowl by a careless slip of a knife.

Chapter Five
Patterns

Most of these spoon patterns have flat, not curved, handles. In most cases side views of these spoons do not add any instructional value and can be confusing. Therefore they are not included. For the curved handle designs or where designs can be better explained, side views have been drawn.

All the spoons in this pattern section are labeled for beginner, intermediate or advanced carvers. If this is your first spoon carving, be sure to choose a beginner pattern. The more intricate intermediate and advanced patterns, though they may look intriguing, may only serve to frustrate a beginning spoon carver.

Many different kinds of woods can be used to carve spoons. Beginning carvers will want to choose a soft wood, like basswood. More experienced carvers may want to try one of the woods listed on page 16. You'll need a block of wood 4" wide by 11" long and $1/2$" to $1 1/2$" deep. The grain should run lengthwise.

Enjoy carving the spoons featured in this pattern section, but don't be afraid to alter them to your own liking. The possibilities for many beautiful spoons are endless.

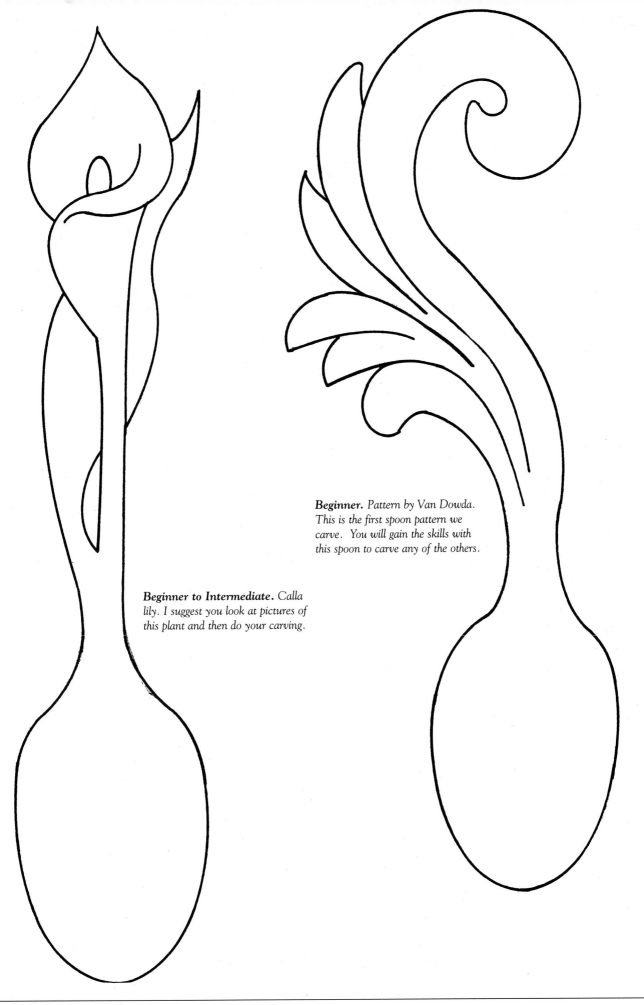

Beginner. *Pattern by Van Dowda. This is the first spoon pattern we carve. You will gain the skills with this spoon to carve any of the others.*

Beginner to Intermediate. *Calla lily. I suggest you look at pictures of this plant and then do your carving.*

Carving Spoons

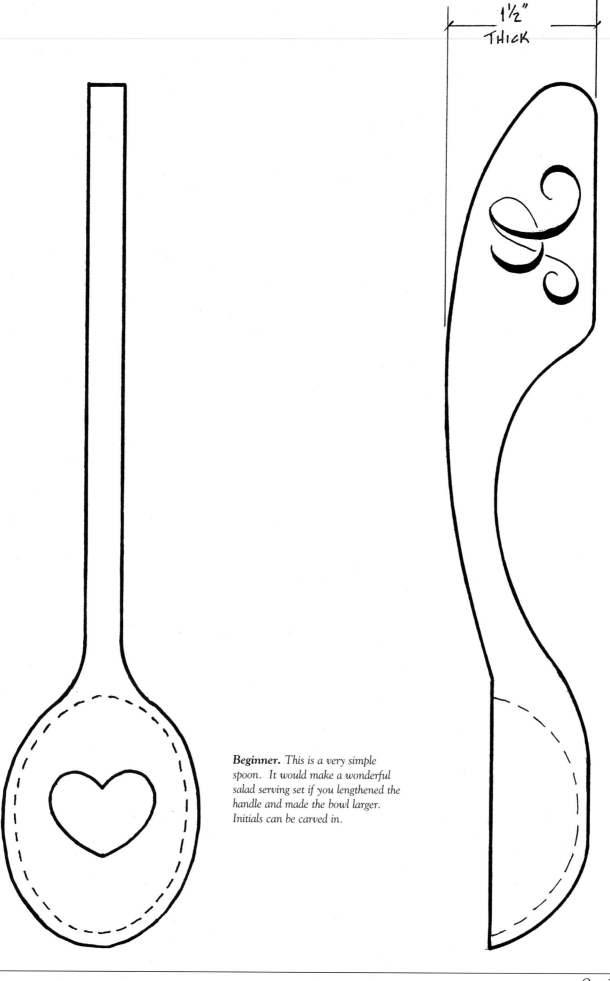

1½"
THICK

Beginner. *This is a very simple spoon. It would make a wonderful salad serving set if you lengthened the handle and made the bowl larger. Initials can be carved in.*

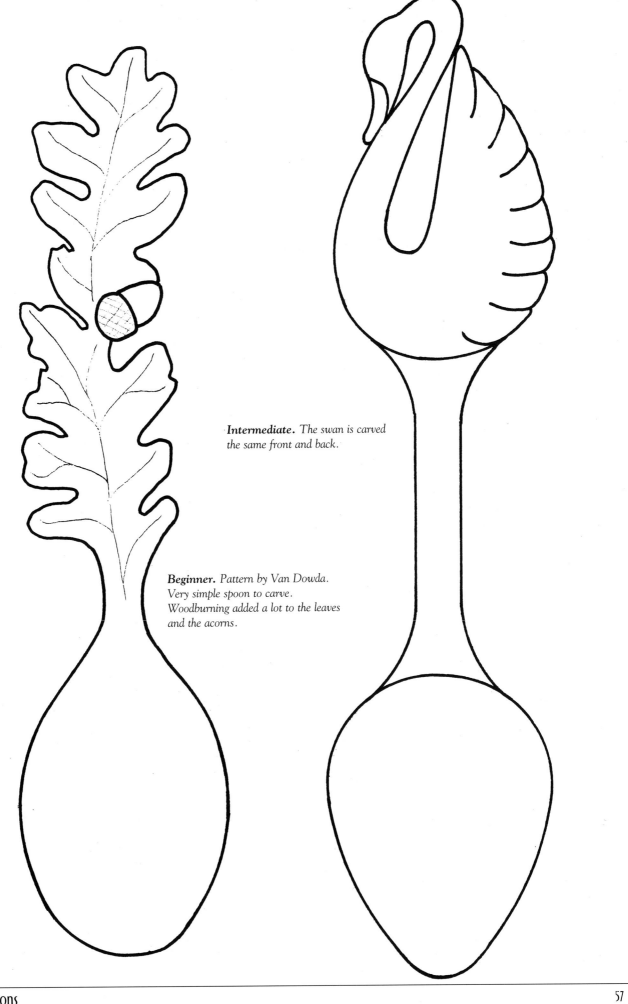

Intermediate. The swan is carved the same front and back.

Beginner. Pattern by Van Dowda. Very simple spoon to carve. Woodburning added a lot to the leaves and the acorns.

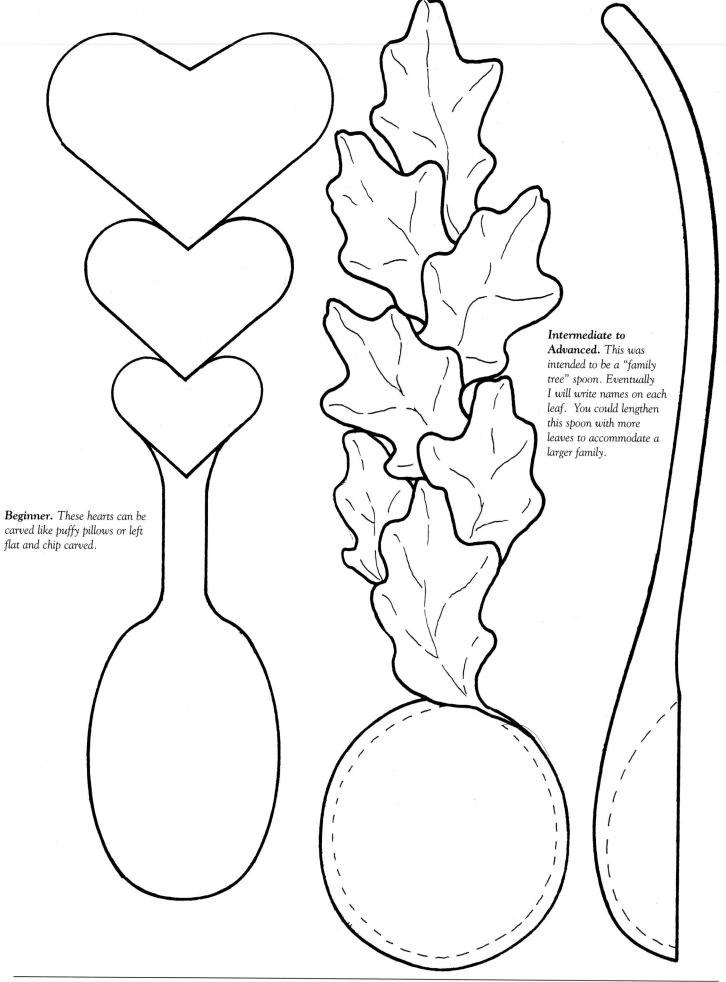

Beginner. These hearts can be carved like puffy pillows or left flat and chip carved.

Intermediate to Advanced. This was intended to be a "family tree" spoon. Eventually I will write names on each leaf. You could lengthen this spoon with more leaves to accommodate a larger family.

Carving Spoons

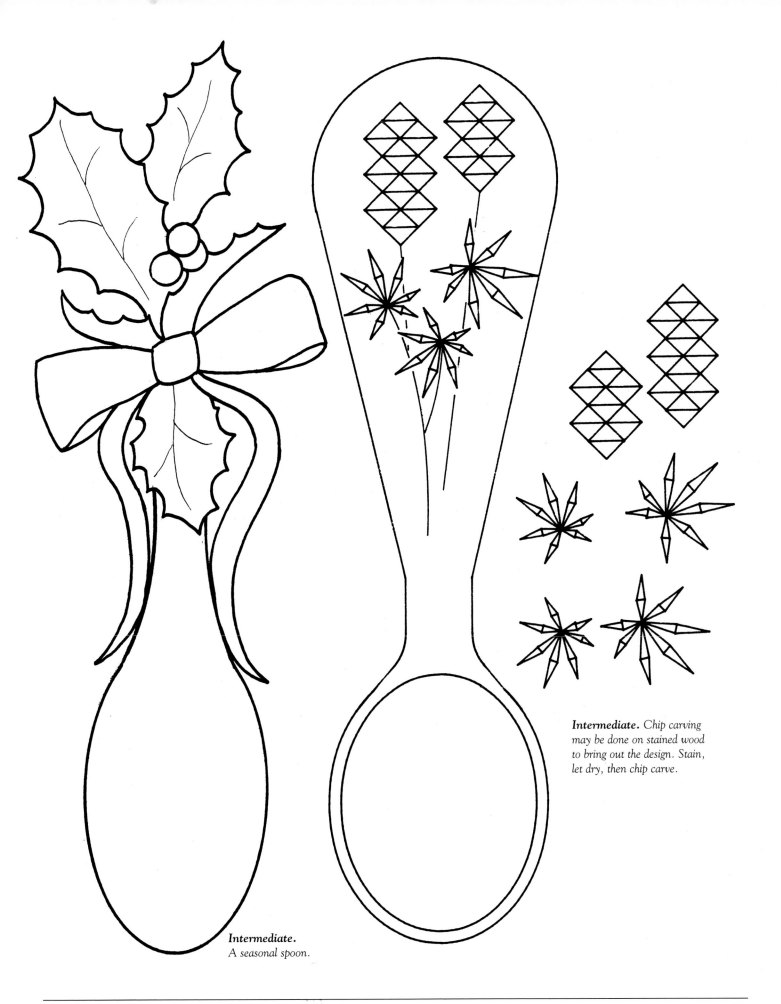

Intermediate. Chip carving may be done on stained wood to bring out the design. Stain, let dry, then chip carve.

Intermediate.
A seasonal spoon.

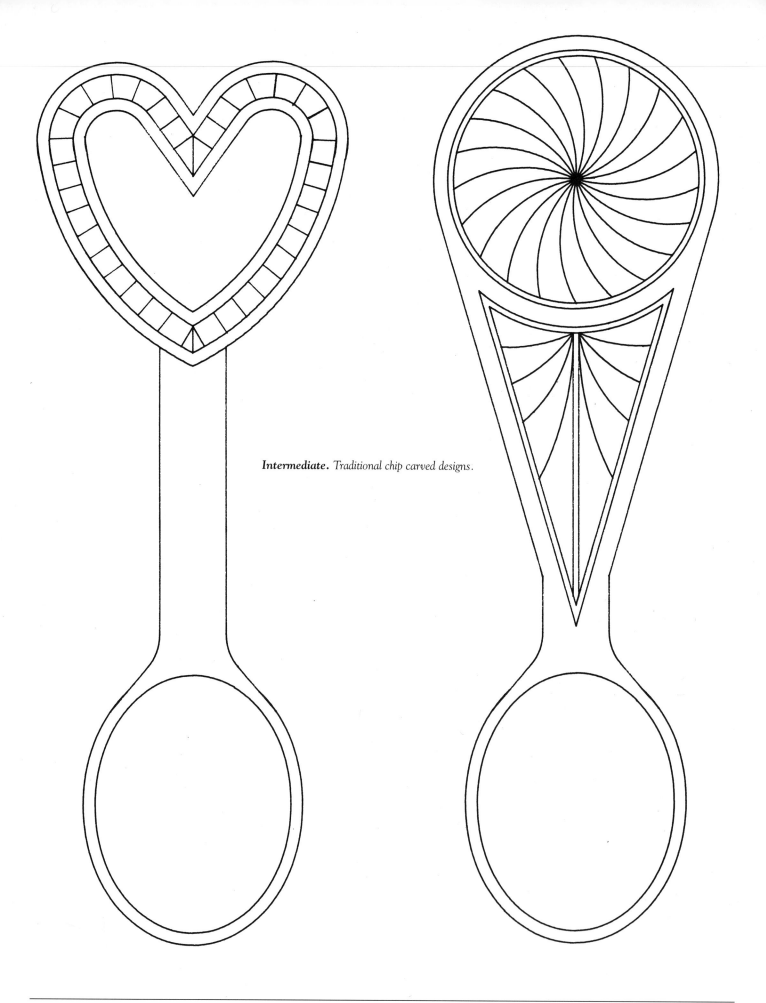

Intermediate. *Traditional chip carved designs.*

Carving Spoons

Intermediate. *Carve a spoon for your favorite musician. Change the bowl shape as desired. A violin, cello, and guitar are included here.*

Intermediate to Advanced. A freeform chip-carved spoon. Sand the handle smooth, stain and let dry, then chip carve.

Intermediate to Advanced. Piercecarving.

Carving Spoons

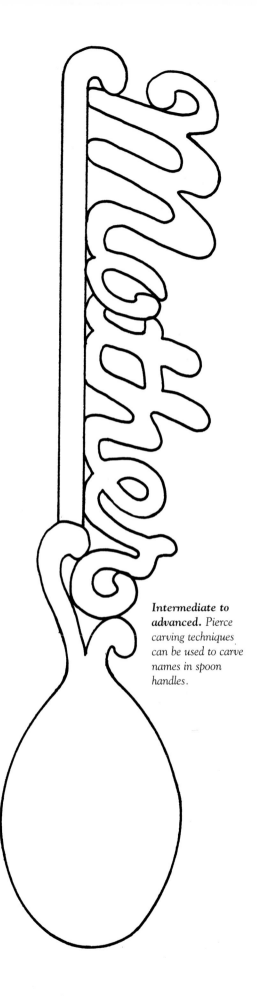

Intermediate to advanced. *Pierce carving techniques can be used to carve names in spoon handles.*

Intermediate to advanced. *Another pierce carved design.*

Intermediate to advanced.
A pierce carved design.

Advanced. A challenge.

Carving Spoons

Advanced. *Reminiscent of Celtic knotwork.*

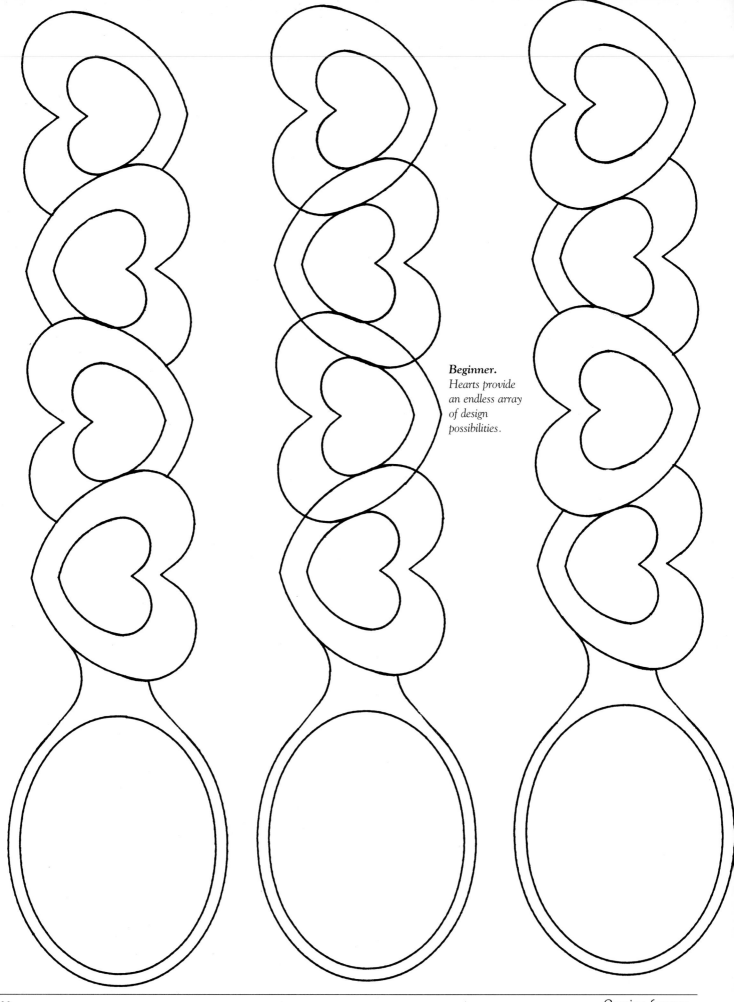

Beginner.
Hearts provide
an endless array
of design
possibilities.

Carving Spoons

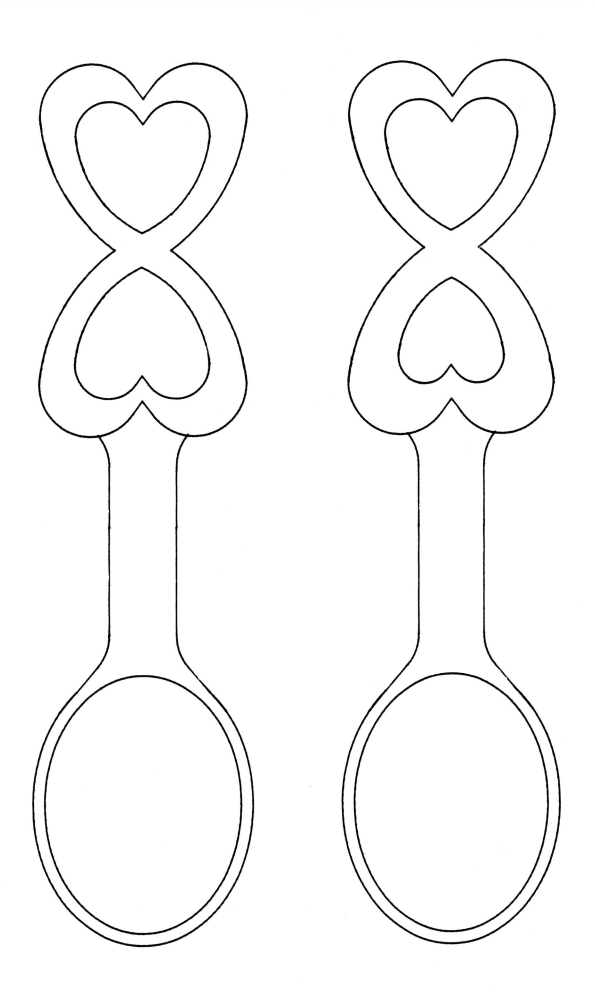

Carving Spoons

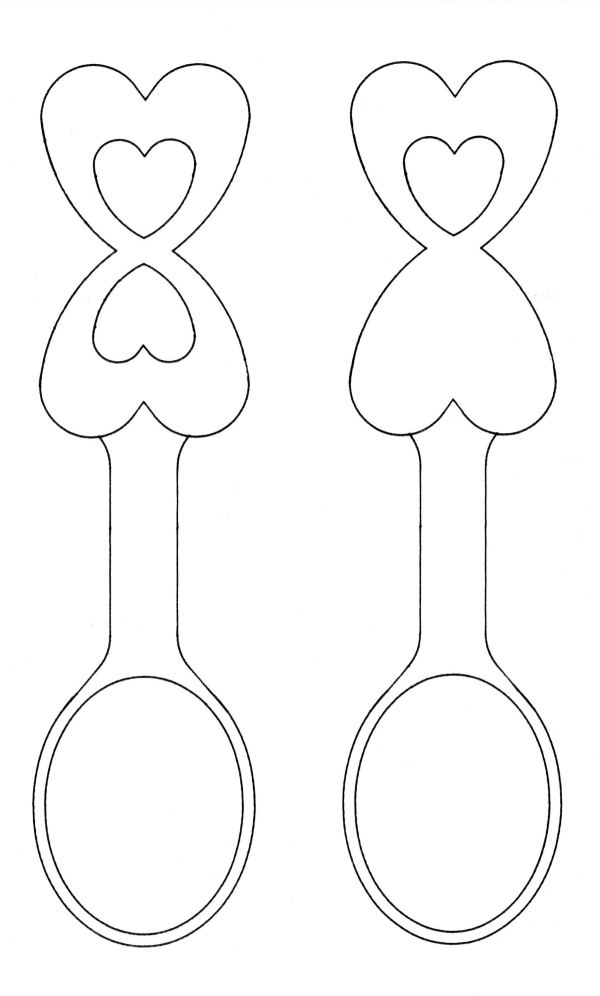

Intermediate. *A series of heart spoons showing how you can have one design and change it to get different spoon handles.*

Carving Spoons

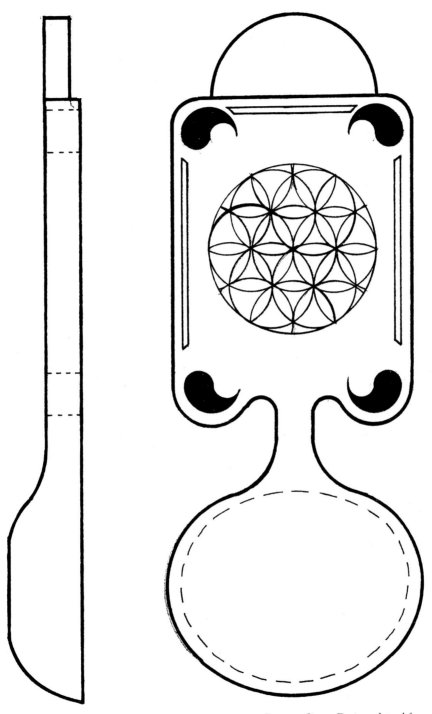

Intermediate. Design adapted from traditional Welsh spoons. Chip carved center design with pierced "comma" corners.

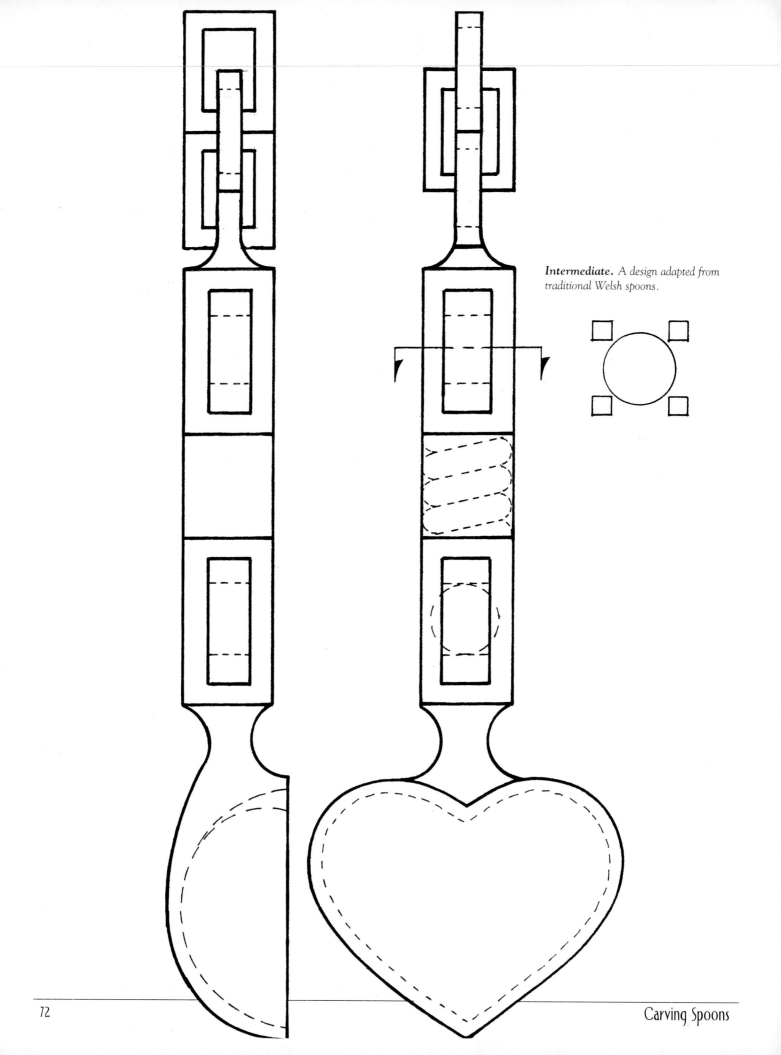

Intermediate. A design adapted from traditional Welsh spoons.

Carving Spoons

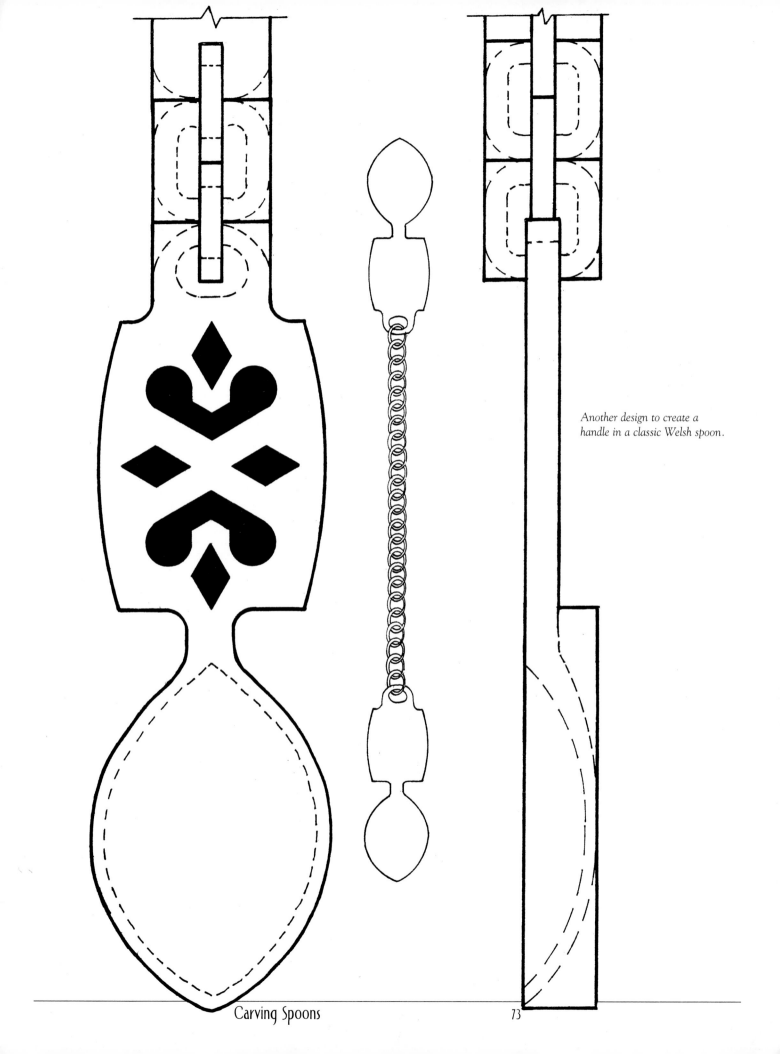

Another design to create a
handle in a classic Welsh spoon.

Carving Spoons

73

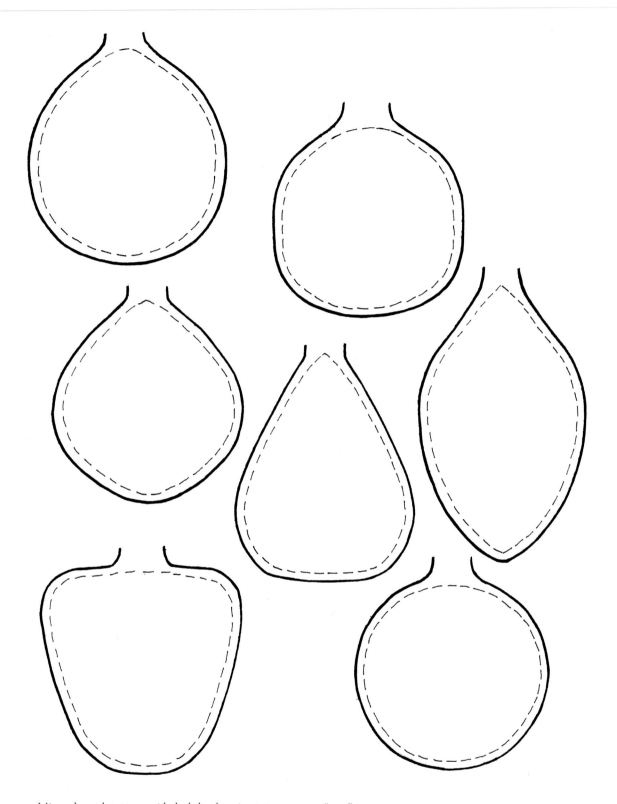

Mix and match patterns with the help of tracing paper to create "new" patterns.

Carving Spoons

Afterword

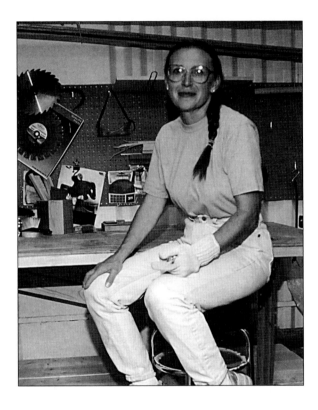

I hope you have enjoyed this introduction to carving spoons. Now that you know that the possibilities are truly endless, I hope you will continue to enjoy spoon carving on your own. Here are three tips to help keep you going.

1. Carve safely.
2. Always try new things....new types of wood, new techniques and new tools.
3. Share your carving with someone else. No matter how inexperienced you feel, you have something to share with others.